# HELPING YOUR CHILD WITH FEARS AND WORRIES

## A Self-Help Guide for Parents

Cathy Creswell and Lucy Willetts

ROBINSON

ROBINSON

First published in Great Britain in 2019 by Robinson

1 3 5 7 9 10 8 6 4 2

The moral rights of the authors have been asserted.

**Important Note**
This book is not intended as a substitute for medical advice or
treatment. Any person with a condition requiring medical attention
should consult a qualified medical practitioner or suitable therapist.

A CIP catalogue record for this book is available from
the British Library

ISBN: 978-1-47213-861-3

Designed and typeset by Initial Typesetting Services, Edinburgh
Printed and bound in Great Britain by Clays Ltd, Elcograf S.p.A.

Papers used by Robinson are from well-managed forests and
other responsible sources

Robinson
An imprint of
Little, Brown Book Group
Carmelite House
50 Victoria Embankment
London EC4Y 0DZ

An Hachette UK Company
www.hachette.co.uk

www.littlebrown.co.uk

# HELPING YOUR CHILD WITH FEARS AND WORRIES

# Contents

## PART III:
### Addressing Particular Needs

# Preface

Anxiety, fears and worries are normal experiences that we all have from time to time, but in some cases they persist and start to interfere in our lives – for children this may bring problems at home, at school and/or with friends. Many children experience problems with anxiety, yet, for parents and carers, it is often difficult to know what to do for the best. Your instincts might be telling you one thing, you may have found different advice on the internet, and other people may have told you to do something else entirely – 'Just ignore him', 'Make her do it', 'Don't give in to it', 'Don't upset him'. This can cause confusion for parents and lead them to doubt themselves and their abilities – but we know that parents can do a fantastic job in helping their children to overcome problems with anxiety.

In this book we aim to give a clear, straightforward step-by-step approach to help you to help your child, based on up-to-date relevant research and our clinical experience of working with hundreds of families who have experienced similar difficulties.

The general approach that we follow is based on the principles of cognitive behavioural therapy (CBT). We will explain this in simple terms throughout the book, but for now we want to let you know that this is the 'gold standard' (or most recommended) approach for overcoming child anxiety problems. Importantly, the approach that we describe in this book has undergone testing in research studies, in which we, and other researchers, have shown that it can be highly effective.

Before we begin, it feels important for us to acknowledge that we know many parents feel a lot of guilt around their child's problems with anxiety. In our clinical work parents often ask us if they have somehow caused the problems or made them worse. So we want to be clear up front that anxiety problems are rarely caused by one single thing and that there are many different factors that can cause childhood anxiety to develop, some of which we will discuss in **Part One** of this book. However, we know that parents are generally desperate to know how to help their child overcome their difficulties and the good news is that they are in a fantastic position to do so.

## Who are we?

We are both clinical psychologists who specialise in working with children and their families. We have worked together since 2004, when we ran a specialist childhood anxiety clinic at the University of Reading which combined the research expertise of university-based personnel with the clinical expertise of National Health Service clinicians. Cathy continues to work at the University of Reading, where she is now a Professor of Developmental Clinical Psychology and leads the Anxiety and Depression in children and Young people (AnDY) research unit and clinic. Lucy now works in private practice and also provides training and supervision in this approach to a range of professionals. In our clinical work we both often help children by working through parents, as we have found that we can get great outcomes for children by supporting parents to build both their own and their child's skills and confidence.

## Who is this book for?

This book is aimed at parents or carers of children who are experiencing difficulties with anxiety. Where there is more than one parent or carer it is of course wonderful if everyone involved can read the book and work together on helping the child. We appreciate that this can sometimes be challenging, and if it is not possible it certainly doesn't need to get in the way of success, so please don't be put off.

We have written this book for parents of primary school age children, roughly 5 to 12 years of age; however, we have added extra chapters towards the end of the book for parents of both younger and older children. The approach can be used with children with a range of anxiety problems – these might include fears and worries about social situations, separating from carers, specific things (such as dogs or spiders), or more general worries about bad things happening.

Two slightly different types of problems are where children experience problematic anxiety and other symptoms after experiencing a traumatic event (which may reflect post-traumatic stress) and where children experience unwanted and intrusive thoughts that drive them to do particular things over and over again (which may reflect obsessive compulsive disorder). While some of the principles in this book may be useful for these conditions, the approach has not been developed to focus on these sorts of difficulties nor been tested with them – if you are concerned that your child might be experiencing these, we would encourage you to contact your GP to identify more targeted support. We are often asked whether the approach will be useful for children with autistic spectrum disorders. Again, while some of the principles may be useful, we have not tested the approach with children with autistic spectrum disorders, so would again encourage you to seek additional support if it is needed.

## What is in this book?

This book is split into three parts – in **Part One** we will tell you about fears, worries and anxiety, including what anxiety problems typically look like, how anxiety problems develop, and the reasons behind the approach we have taken in this book. In **Part Two** we take you through step-by-step techniques to help you help your child to overcome their problems with fears, worries and anxiety. In **Part Three** we address some specific issues that might be relevant to some (but not all) readers: using this book with younger children, using this book with teenagers, sleep problems, difficult behaviour, school attendance difficulties. Finally, we have also included a brief guide that can be copied and passed on to teachers or other school staff where it would be helpful for them to be able to understand and support the approach you are taking.

Throughout this book we will be talking you through principles to help you to spot patterns or vicious cycles that your child may have become stuck in, and sharing skills and strategies either to break these cycles or prevent them from occurring. Along the way you will read about other parents' experiences of living with an anxious child and how they helped their child to overcome their fears and worries. These stories are based on real families that we have worked with; however, names and details have been changed to prevent identification.

By sharing information, strategies and others' experiences, our aim is to put you and your child back in control of your lives. We wish you all the very best with everything you are doing to make this happen.

# PART I

◇◇◇◇◇◇◇◇◇◇◇◇

# Understanding Your Child's Fears and Worries

1

# What are fears, worries and anxiety?

Although it may be tempting to skip this section and get stuck straight into working on changing things, we want to strongly encourage you to take the time to read through these first five brief chapters before you start to read Part Two. There are three main reasons for this. First, chapters 1, 2 and 3 describe the problem of fears, worries and anxiety in children. By reading them you will be able to make sure that this is the right book for you, in the sense that it is focused on the problem that you want to work on with your child (or encourage someone else to work on with their child).

Second, chapters 4 and 5 explain how fears and worries develop in young people and what keeps these fears and worries going. The information given in these chapters provides the rationale for all the work you will do when you follow the guide in Part Two. Having a clear understanding of why you are doing what you are doing will make it much easier for you to put the strategies in place and will encourage you to persevere when the going is tough.

Third, in Part One you will be introduced to four children: Ben (aged 9), Muhammed (7), Layla (11) and Sarah (10). These children have all experienced fears and worries, and in Part One you will hear some of the background to their difficulties, before reading in Part Two about how their parents helped them to overcome these. We appreciate that you will be keen to get going with the central theme of the book – the actual overcoming of fear and worries – and we have therefore kept Part One brief. Please do read on.

## What do we mean by fears, worries and anxiety?

Everyone, children and adults alike, experiences worries, fears and anxiety some of the time. What worries, fears and anxiety have in common is that they involve an expectation that something bad is going to happen, a particular way in which our bodies respond to this, and certain characteristic behaviours.

### Anxious thinking/expectations

When people become anxious they typically expect that something bad is about to happen. At this time thoughts tend to become focused on the potential threat and how to escape from it, and it can be hard to think about anything else. This is clearly a useful state to be in when someone is in danger. For example, if your child is about to step into the road you need to be focused on getting them out of the way of oncoming traffic and not be easily distracted by other thoughts, such as what you need to buy at the shops or what you are having for dinner.

## Bodily changes

When we experience fears and worries, we respond in a number of ways. These include our breathing getting faster, heart rate speeding up, muscles becoming tense, sweating and 'butterflies' in the tummy. All of these bodily signs represent our body getting ready for action, enabling us to react quickly, such as, in the above example, pulling the child out of the way before he or she comes to any harm.

## Anxious behaviour

The way we behave in response to fears or worries is often categorised as either 'fight', 'flight' or 'safety-seeking': we either fight against the threat, get out of the way as quickly as we can (take flight), or do other things that we think will keep us safe.

When we are faced with immediate threats these are, of course, the most helpful ways to respond and can be essential for our survival, but when there is no objective danger these thoughts, feelings and behaviours can cause difficulties and get in the way of day-to-day life.

## So how do I know if my child's anxiety is excessive?

The changes that we experience in response to anxiety are helpful in the short term, but if these reactions continue to occur when actual danger has passed, or when, in fact, it was never there, they become problematic. When anxiety is excessive, thinking can become dominated by fearing the worst: your child may always seem to expect the worst to happen and lack confidence in their ability to cope with challenges. Bodily changes can also be very uncomfortable. Children who are highly anxious often complain of tummy aches, headaches or muscle aches.

Finally, when anxiety persists, not only is it exhausting to feel constantly 'on edge' but also trying to keep safe can lead your child to miss out on doing things that they would otherwise enjoy. If fears and worries are getting in the way of your child enjoying themselves or being able to do the things that other children of the same age are doing, then it is important that they are helped to overcome these difficulties. This book is about giving you the tools to help your child to do just that.

As we have seen, a certain amount of fear and worry is both normal and healthy, so the aim of this book is not to help you to get your child to a point where they *never* worry or are *never* scared of anything. Instead, our aim is to assist you in helping your child take control of their fears and worries so that they do not get in the way of them getting the most out of life.

When children with anxiety problems receive appropriate treatment, they generally do very well. There is a lot of information in this book, but the central message is simple: anxiety problems are extremely common among children, they can interfere with your child's life, and they *can* be overcome.

---

**Key points**

- Anxiety is a normal emotion that everyone experiences at times

- When we are anxious we have anxious expectations, bodily signs, and engage in anxious behaviour

- The approach in this book can stop anxiety interfering in your child's everyday life

# 2

# How can I help my child?

The fact that you are reading this book shows that you are keen and motivated to help your child. However, you are probably also feeling quite daunted by the prospect. You will no doubt have tried many things to help your child in the past and have probably received all sorts of different advice from different people along the way. You may well feel like you have tried everything you can and may not feel very confident that there is anything further you can do. These sorts of experiences and concerns are very common among the parents we work with. But there are a number of reasons why we would encourage you to work with your child on overcoming their anxiety. We have listed some of these below:

- Where parents can help their child overcome their difficulties, this reduces the burden on children to attend appointments with professionals within schools or the health service, meaning children don't miss out on other age-appropriate activities that they could be doing.

- Parents are often in a better position than therapists to put strategies in place and to create opportunities for new learning in their child's day-to-day life.

- Parents are often more motivated than the child to make changes, as children may be more focused on the short-term pain whereas parents are likely to be more focused on the long-term gain!

- Parents can sometimes put the strategies in place across the family, potentially helping other children (and sometimes adults) within the family.

- Parents are more likely to remember what has been helpful in the months and years that follow and so are in a great position to put these strategies in place in the future if problems come up again.

- Parents are often the ones having to manage their child's difficulties on a day-to-day basis. This can be enormously stressful, and parents tell us that they want strategies to help them know what to do.

For all these reasons we believe that parents are in a strong and unique position to help their children overcome fears and worries. The aim of this book is to help you to feel skilled and confident in how to do this.

## Does it work?

In recent years there have been a number of studies that have tested out treatments for children with anxiety disorders in which parents are supported in helping their child, and where the child is not seen by the therapist at all. In these studies, parents of 5- to 12-year-old children are typically given a book like this and are supported by a therapist in putting the strategies it contains in place. Often the therapist's role is to help keep the parent focused on using the strategies within their busy lives, but the therapist might also provide opportunities to practise particular strategies or problem-solve any difficulties that arise. These studies have shown that this is an effective treatment approach, and in some cases, it has been as effective as far more intensive family-focused treatments in which the child and parent attend regular sessions with a therapist. If you would like to read more about these research studies, we have included information about how to access them in the Key references section at the end of the book.

## What if it doesn't work?

Our experience suggests that using this book with your child over around two months can lead to huge progress within that time. For some, initial improvements may be slower and happen in the months that follow. So, if you do not see change straight away do not give up.

If, however, on finishing working through the book you feel you need more support, then we would strongly advise you to seek help via your GP or school. They can advise on services available to you locally that can support you in applying the principles in this book or offer other approaches depending on the difficulties your child is experiencing. We know that parents can be reluctant to seek help for their child for many reasons. For example:

• They may feel that they will be judged in some way

• They think they *should* be able to manage the difficulties within their own family

• They think it is not a medical doctor's job to deal with these sorts of problems.

However, it is important to recognise that these sorts of difficulties are common, they are experienced by all sorts of different families with all sorts of different backgrounds, that effective treatments are available, and that GPs will often see children with these sorts of difficulties and will be able to help you access support. So, if you are concerned, please do ask for help.

**Key points**

- You are in a unique position to help your child overcome their fears and worries

- Our research suggests working through parents to help children is effective

- Seek help through your child's GP or school if you find you need additional support

# 3

# Common fears and worries experienced by children

All children will experience fears and worries in different ways, and while using this book it is important for you to try to get a clear understanding of your child's unique experience. Every family we work with describes an experience that we have not heard about before. However, they also have a great deal in common with other families. The basic patterns of anxious thinking, behaviour and physical symptoms have been described in Chapter 1; however, we can also group certain types of anxiety problems together based on more specific features or symptoms. These groups of anxiety problems have been given labels called 'diagnoses'. The most common categories of anxiety problems among children are: specific phobias, social anxiety, generalised anxiety, and separation anxiety. These different sorts of difficulties often go hand in hand. In fact, among the children we work with, seeing a child who has just one of these types of anxiety is the exception rather than the rule. We describe what is meant by each of these categories below.

## Specific phobias

When a fear of a particular place, object or situation becomes a problem it is called a phobia. This describes a fear that is excessive and leads to avoidance or extreme discomfort when a child is faced with the feared object (or place or situation). Fears are common; a lot of people are cautious of, for example, snakes or bees and this can be a healthy response. If, however, your child's fear is significantly interfering with his or her life, such as causing problems at school, in the family or with friends, or if it stops him or her from doing things he or she would like to do, then it would no doubt be best for your child to receive help in overcoming this fear. Common fears we see in children include fears of dogs, heights, injections and vomiting.

### *Sarah (aged 10)*

*Sarah has never liked spiders. I remember when she was just a toddler she once became hysterical because she saw a bit of fluff on the carpet which looked a bit like a spider. Since then she has always had to keep away if we came across a spider in the room, but it never used to cause a big problem. Over time it just seems to have got worse. Now we're finding that there are certain places that Sarah won't want to go to because she thinks we're likely to see a spider. For example, her granddad had to*

*go into hospital for a month, so his flat was empty for all*
*that time. We went over to give it a clean-up before he*
*came home. We shouldn't have taken Sarah with us really*
*because, not surprisingly, we came across a spider before*
*too long. Sarah got really upset and was out the door*
*before you could do anything about it. Since then she has*
*refused to go back to her granddad's house, so he always*
*has to come to us to visit, which feels unfair on him.*

## Social anxiety

When a child is socially anxious they are typically anxious about a variety of different situations in which they fear doing something embarrassing, that people will think they are stupid, judge them negatively, or react badly to them. For children this can make it difficult to enter into situations where there will be other people – for example, going to school, being with other children (such as at parties), and going to cafes or restaurants. It may also make it hard for a child to participate in a social situation, for example, not being able to put their hand up in class or talk in a large group of peers. Although children who are socially anxious may be perfectly comfortable when they are with people they know well, they may try to avoid situations where there will be less familiar people or may feel very uncomfortable if they have to be in these kinds of situations. Occasionally, when social anxiety is severe, children are not able to talk at all in certain situations such as at school or with people outside of their home. This is commonly referred to as 'selective mutism'.

### Layla (aged 11)

*Layla's biggest problem is with school. In the summer holidays she's like a different person. Then maybe a week before she's due to go back she'll start getting the tummy aches. It's the same on a Sunday evening during the school term. It's really hard to know if she is genuinely ill or not, especially as sometimes she is physically sick, and she tends to go white as a sheet at the mention of going to school. This problem has been around for a while although, when she was ten, she had a really support-ive teacher and things seemed to settle down for a bit. But since she has changed class, she has found it really hard. She seems to think everybody thinks badly of her. So, any little thing will upset her, like if another child is just looking at her she'll think they are thinking there is something wrong with her hair or her clothes. Her teach-ers have told me that she is really quiet in class and never puts her hand up or tries to participate. She often comes home with no idea of what she should be doing for her homework as she hasn't understood it but hasn't asked the teacher what to do.*

# Generalised anxiety

Generalised anxiety describes a condition where a child worries excessively and finds it hard to get worries out of his or her mind. The worries tend to be about a range of different concerns, rather than a single issue. For example, common worries can include things going on in the world (such as terrorism), doing well at school, friendships, getting things right, and the health of ourselves and others. For some children, the worries change over time, so a child can move from worrying about one thing to something else. The worries are often accompanied by unpleasant physical symptoms such as difficulty concentrating, muscle aches, sleep problems (difficulty settling or frequent waking), irritability and tiredness. Again, these difficulties can interfere with the child's ability to enjoy activities at home, school, in the family or with friends. Generalised anxiety can present a bit differently from some of the other anxiety problems – with more worry and less avoidance – and for this reason there are some particular strategies that work well (see Chapter 12).

### Ben (aged 9)

*The best way to describe Ben is as 'a worrier'. He seems to worry about anything and everything. I have stopped putting the news on when he is around because it is like he is on the lookout for bad news. For example, he is terrified that we are all going to catch the illness that has been talked about on the news that is happening on the other side of the world. He also gets really wound up when his dad has to go into the city for work as he has seen stories about bombs and terrorism.*

*I suppose I can understand those worries, but there are others I find harder. He just gets something into his head and it seems to get stuck there. Like he has a real worry about a monster that was in a film that he watched at his cousin's house. He is convinced that if he goes upstairs the monster is going to come and get him, to the point that he won't go upstairs on his own. We tell him that there is no monster, it was just a made-up character, and just to forget about it, but he just can't seem to get rid of this thought. Since this has been going on he has had to share a bedroom with his brother, but it takes Ben so long to get to sleep at night because he is worrying about something or other that this is now disturbing his brother's sleep, too.*

## Separation anxiety

Some children find it extremely difficult to be apart from a parent or other carer. This often relates to a fear that if they are separated from their carer they will not see each other again. This can either be because of a fear that some harm will come to the child if their carer is not present (such as they will get taken or injured), or that harm will come to their carer in the child's absence. These fears can make it difficult for a child to take part in a range of activities that other children of the same age will be doing, including attending school, visiting friends, going to after-school clubs or activities, or going on sleepovers.

### *Muhammed (aged 7)*

*There are a lot of things Muhammed finds difficult, but I think the one I struggle with the most is bedtime. Muhammed needs to have me or his dad there with him for him to go to sleep. We feel like we have tried everything – we have insisted he stay in his room and have let him cry, but he just got himself so worked up that it seemed to make things worse; we decorated his room for him so that it would be a nice place to be – none of these things have made any difference. What tends to happen is that one of us will go in with Muhammed and read him a story and then we have to lie down on his bed with him until he drops off. Quite often we'll end up dropping off, too, then we lose a big chunk of our evening. Then when we finally do get to bed, more often than not we'll be woken up to find Muhammed has crept in, too, at some point in the night. I think the fact that none of us are getting enough sleep is making everything*

*else harder to deal with. The other big thing is, of course,
school. Muhammed has missed a great deal of school this
year as he just finds it so difficult, and we just don't have
the energy to keep pushing him to go any more. It just
doesn't seem like it can be good for him to go through so
much stress each day. I try to imagine him ten years from
now. He certainly can't be coming in to our bed then.
Something has to be done.*

## How common are anxiety problems in children?

Anxiety problems are the most common form of emotional
and behavioural problems experienced by young people.
Studies have estimated that about 6.5 per cent of children
worldwide meet criteria for a diagnosis of an 'anxiety disorder'. By that we mean a level of anxiety that is leading to
high levels of distress and/or is causing them to miss out
on age-appropriate opportunities. In other words, more
than one in every twenty children is likely to have an anxiety problem that gets in the way of their day-to-day life.
In terms of particular types of anxiety disorders, findings
vary across studies, but phobias have been found to affect
up to a quarter of children, and other anxiety disorders
like separation anxiety disorder can affect up to one in five
children. Separation anxiety disorder is more commonly
found among pre-adolescent children than adolescents;

and social anxiety disorder is more common among adolescents than pre-adolescent children.

# The effects on children's lives

## The effects on social life

### *Muhammed*

*Muhammed is at an age now where his friends are starting to sleep over at each other's houses and go away to camps and things like that. We've tried to get Muhammed along to an after-school football club, but he'll only join in if he knows he will be able to see me at all times. He has a 'school journey' coming up next term where they will stay away for three nights. I think there is no way he will be able to go. I feel like he is really missing out and I worry that his friends are going to lose interest as he gets older if Mum or Dad are always hanging about.*

It is easy to see how certain anxiety problems can affect children's developing social lives. Throughout childhood, friendships are essential for children to learn and practise what they need to know to form lasting relationships. They also provide an essential reference point for children to discover that many of the challenges they experience are quite normal. Friends also, of course, provide opportunities for fun, and encourage and motivate each other to try new experiences. Throughout childhood and adolescence, relationships between friends are constantly changing. When anxiety causes a child to withdraw from their friends at school or other social opportunities a vicious cycle can form, because changes that have occurred within their group of friends make it harder for the child to join it again, as shown in the diagram below.

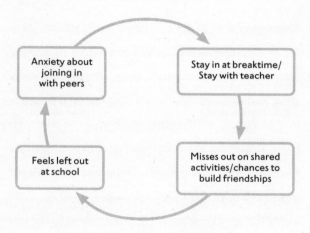

Figure 3.1 Vicious cycle created when child
withdraws at school

## The effects on academic performance

There is no reason to think that children who have problems with anxiety are any less bright than children who do not have anxiety problems. Despite this, children with anxiety problems do tend to experience more academic problems. This is likely to be because their anxiety is preventing them from achieving their full potential. Again, a vicious cycle can develop in which not asking for help, difficulties concentrating and taking in new information, or even missing lessons caused by worry in the classroom leads to problems with school, which in turn leads to greater anxiety about being able to get the work done, as shown in the diagrams that follow.

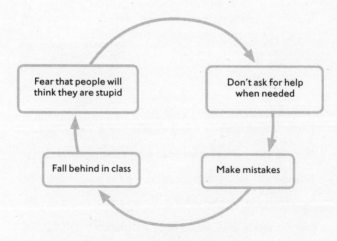

Figure 3.2 Vicious cycle created when a child is anxious about seeking help at school

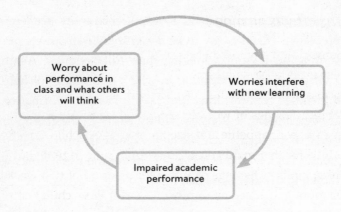

Figure 3.3 Vicious cycle created when anxiety interferes with memory and concentration at school

## *Layla*

*Layla is now having a real problem at school. The fact that she misses more days from school than most children because she makes herself so ill isn't a good start. She has always struggled a bit with her work, but it is just getting worse and worse now, as she isn't getting the help she needs because she never lets the teacher know that she needs it. She also says that she can't remember what the teacher has asked her to do, as her mind was full with worries about things going wrong.*

## The effects on mood

Some children who experience significant anxiety problems also experience symptoms of low mood or depression, such as loss of interest in their usual activities, tearfulness or irritability, feelings of worthlessness, and physical symptoms such as poor appetite and sleep problems. All children (and adults for that matter) feel down from time to time, but if these kinds of feelings continue for a period of two weeks or more and it seems impossible to lift your child out of this low mood then it will be important to address this. The strategies that are described in Part Two of this book are useful skills for life and can be helpful for overcoming mild to moderate low mood. If this applies to your child, you may find that by helping them to overcome their fears or worries they will begin to feel better about themself and be more able to participate in activities that they find fulfilling. However, if your child is extremely withdrawn and lacking in motivation, you may find it difficult to apply some of the strategies that we will introduce you to. In this case we would recommend you visit your GP to discuss ways that you and your child could access greater support to help improve their mood before embarking on this programme.

### Ben

*Ben just seems to have the weight of the world on his shoulders. It seems like such a rare occurrence that I see him laugh or smile. It makes me really sad to think that such a young boy feels that way. Other children his age seem to be laughing and joking without a care. I just wish he could be the same way.*

## Will my child grow out of this problem?

Studies that have kept in touch with children with anxiety disorders over time have tended to report that symptoms can persist for several years. When we consider the effects that anxiety problems can have on children's social lives, academic performance and mood, this presents a gloomy picture. On the other hand, it is important to stress that treatments for childhood anxiety have excellent success rates. The clear implication of this is that if your child is experiencing anxiety problems then it is important that this is recognised and dealt with.

---

**Key points**

- Around 5–10 per cent of children meet the criteria for an anxiety disorder

- Common anxiety disorders in children are separation, social and generalised anxiety disorder, and specific phobias

- Fears and worries can impact on a child's social life, academic performance and mood

- Many children overcome their problems with anxiety with the sort of support we describe in this book

---

# 4

# How do fears and worries develop in children?

## *Ben*

*Ben has always been a worrier. He always seems to see and fear the worst happening. I see other children his age and these kinds of thoughts don't even seem to cross their minds. I do think a lot about what must have caused it. On the one hand it seems like he has always been a bit this way. Even when he was a baby he seemed jumpy and found it really hard to relax. It was always a real job to get him to sleep at night. There are other people who worry a lot in my family, so I guess that must be a part of it. He has also had a lot to cope with in his life so far. He lost two grandparents whom he was very close to within a year and that was very upsetting for him. But I also can't help thinking, 'Is it something that we've done?', 'Have we made him this way somehow?'*

The majority of parents whom we have worked with have been keen to get a better understanding of why their child has difficulties with fears and worries. This is partly to enable them to help their child overcome these fears and worries, but it is sometimes also because parents worry that they are in some way to blame for their child's anxiety. Parents certainly can influence how anxious their child is or isn't in particular situations (and if they couldn't, there would be no point to a book like this!). It is rare, however, for a child's fears and worries to be caused by any one thing. A child's anxiety level and the extent that this interferes with their life are, instead, generally a result of a variety of influences. This chapter will talk you through the most common factors: (i) genetics and inherited personality characteristics; and (ii) learning experiences, including what is learned from other people and specific life events.

## What do we inherit?

It is well known that we all inherit certain physical characteristics from our parents; for example, eye colour, hair colour, how tall we are and a range of other physical features. The same is true for psychological characteristics. We may inherit a tendency to have a quick temper, be impulsive, or be laid back. You are likely to feel that many of the ways your child responds to things (emotionally or behaviourally) resemble how you or other people in your family also respond (or might have responded when you were children).

It is now also well known that 'anxiety runs in families'. Studies that have assessed family members of children who are anxious have tended to find higher rates of anxiety in parents and siblings than would be explained by chance. In general, research has suggested that there is a genetic influence on anxiety in childhood. Although estimates vary across studies, about one third of the influence on general anxiety seems to be caused by genetics. In simple terms, anxiety is caused by one part genes and two parts experiences.

# Genes vs environment in the development of anxiety

## What exactly is inherited?

Although a child and his or her parent may both be great football players, we wouldn't normally think that this means football playing ability is 'in their genes'. It is quite likely, however, that other characteristics which help someone to be good at football (such as strength, speed and quick reactions) may at least be partly inherited. It is probable that anxiety runs in families in a similar kind of way. Rather than us inheriting a particular anxiety disorder, we are likely to inherit certain characteristics that make us more inclined to become highly anxious at some point in our lives. Two possible things that are inherited are (i) how easily our body jumps to action in response to threat (such as how easily a baby is startled by loud noises), and

(ii) how generally emotional we are (such as how easily a baby becomes distressed).

## The environmental element

At this point you may well be thinking, 'If my child was born this way then what hope do I have of changing it?' This is a common reaction; however, as we have seen, genetics can never fully tell us whether a child is going to develop problems with fears or anxiety. There are a large number of children who may come from a family of 'worriers' but who never experience excessive fear or worry themselves. Similarly, your child may have brothers or sisters who do not appear anxious in the least. There are also many children who may have seemed easily upset as babies, difficult to settle and reserved as toddlers but who go on to experience no problems with fears or worries. Clearly the experiences that the child has in their life have a crucial influence on how fears and worries develop.

### Adverse life events

#### *Muhammed*

*I don't feel that Muhammed has had the best start in life. There has been so much upheaval. I split up from his biological father when he was just a baby and he hasn't really had any consistent contact with him throughout his life.*

*I've been with my partner for most of Muhammed's life,*
*and Muhammed thinks of him as 'Dad', but he has a job*
*that involves him being away a lot of the time. We have*
*also had to move quite a lot for various reasons, includ-*
*ing financial problems, so there has been quite a bit of*
*stress in the family, and Muhammed has changed schools*
*and moved away from his old friends. I guess if I was him*
*maybe I'd be anxious, too.*

As we have said above, many parents report that their child
has always seemed to be fearful or a worrier. But they also
often say that the fears or worries got worse or began to
cause more disruption after a particular life event. It is difficult to know for sure whether people who experience a lot
of fears and worries have had more stressful events happen
in their lives or not. The reason for this is that a stressful
event may have a much bigger impact on an anxious
person than the same event would have on a less anxious
person. Equally, however, for some children difficult experiences can sometimes help them build resilience. You may
be able to think of two children you know who have had
similar difficult life experiences but have responded to
them in completely different ways. It seems that the influence of stressful experiences on children's fears and worries
depends on factors other than the nature of the experience
alone. This can include the child's genetic vulnerability to
anxiety, but also other environmental influences such as
what the child learns from the people around them.

## LEARNING BY EXAMPLE

From a young age, children learn from watching other people around them. Children are likely to rely most heavily on information they get from observing those who are close to them, such as parents or carers, and siblings. In order to survive in the world, it is essential that children learn this way, to help them to stay away from potential danger and harm. This process has very clear advantages. The disadvantage is that children can learn unhelpful responses from those close to them too. Researchers have shown that children who are prone to anxiety seem to pay particular attention to the reactions of people around them and are more easily influenced by this than more laid-back children. In other words, we could act in a very anxious way around some children and it might have no effect on them, whereas a more anxious child is more likely to pay attention to our reactions and take this as further evidence of potential threat. This presents a particular challenge for parents of anxious children.

### *Layla*

*I am doing my best to help Layla get over her fears, but I know I don't always set a very good example. For example, when I used to go with her to the school gates I used to find it really difficult. There are so many other parents there. They all seem to know each other. In that situation*

*I just try to keep my head down and get in and out as quickly as I can.*

Parents are often aware of their own fears and worries and make a conscious effort to cover them up from their children for exactly this reason. Children (particularly those who are prone to anxiety) are highly tuned to their carers' reactions, however, and can be extremely good at picking up subtle signs that something is wrong. For example, Joe (who is discussed in Chapter 16) is scared of dogs. His dad isn't keen on dogs either but makes an effort to hide this fear from Joe. If Joe's dad is walking down the street with Joe and he sees a big dog coming towards them he will contain his fear and calmly cross the road so that he is not put in a situation in which Joe will see him get scared. Nonetheless, from the fact that they have crossed the road Joe has picked up a message from his dad that there is good reason to stay away from dogs.

## LEARNING FROM OTHER PEOPLE'S REACTIONS

As we have described above, many anxious children are naturally more fearful than others and/or they may have had some difficult experiences to cope with. It is not surprising, therefore, that parents may show concern about how their child will cope given their past experience, and try to do their best to prevent their child from becoming distressed. For example, parents may inadvertently encourage their child to avoid situations that they fear.

### *Ben*

*What would I do if Ben asked to go up to London for his birthday? I think I'd fall off my chair! Well, no, I guess I'd be really pleased that he wanted to do that. But I'd be pretty doubtful that he'd make it. He might say he wants to but as the time approaches he would start to worry about it and it would end up just ruining his birthday. I think all I could do really was try to suggest other things when he brought it up – maybe do something local where we don't need to go on public transport or do anything he might see as dangerous.*

Similarly, if a child does enter into a potentially difficult situation, parents may, inadvertently, respond in a way that increases the child's fear. For example, when Joe strokes a dog, does his dad smile and look comfortable, or does he look concerned, serious or uncomfortable? When Layla reads a line in a school assembly, does her mum sit nodding and looking relaxed and confident in Layla's ability, or does she sit on the edge of her chair, wringing her hands, worrying how Layla is going to get on?

The problem with this is that, as well as watching what other people do, anxious children are also on the lookout for how other people react to what they do. To a child who is prone to anxiety, parent reactions such as those described above may suggest that something bad may be about to happen or that their parent has a lack of confidence in their ability to cope. Parents might not necessarily act in ways that are as obvious as those in the examples given, but they may try to reduce their child's distress by: (unintentionally) encouraging the child to avoid his or her fears; stepping in to sort out problems for the child; or giving a lot of reassurance. As we have explained, all of these are completely natural reactions to a child who is distressed. Parents are designed by evolution to protect their children, so this urge to keep them safe and ease their distress is very strong!

Avoiding or removing a child from an anxiety-provoking situation may achieve this aim in the short term. The difficulty is that all of these normal, natural parental behaviours may, in the long term, prevent a child who is very anxious from trying out new situations, developing skills for dealing with these situations, and overcoming the associated worries and fears. This is often the number one challenge for parents of anxious children – the child's fears and worries can lead a parent's protective instincts to kick in and make them respond in particular ways, but because the child is anxious they pay particular attention to these responses – so unfortunately these natural parental reactions can end up keeping the child's anxiety going. So, it's really important that we are aware of when this happens – and at times we need to try and work to resist our natural protective urges and allow children to 'have a go'.

## COPING EXPERIENCES

In order to overcome fears, children need the opportunity to test out their anxious expectations – for example, that something bad will happen or that they will not be able to deal with anxious feelings – and learn that they can cope with these situations. When a parent is extremely concerned about their child becoming anxious and wants to protect them, the child may not get as many opportunities to test out their fears and learn from challenges.

### *Layla*

*When Layla started preschool, it was her first experience of anything like that, so it was really quite hard for her. When she was a little baby I couldn't see what she would get out of going along to groups. It seemed to be more an opportunity for the mums to get together, so I didn't tend to go as I'm not really comfortable with that kind of thing. Then as she got older, toddler age and after that, when we did go into any situation where there would be a big group of people she would just get so upset by it that it seemed better to just keep away. She certainly wasn't enjoying being there and she wasn't getting the benefit of it, as she spent the whole time stuck to me.*

Layla's mum's reaction is understandable and demonstrates another way in which the experiences that we have can result from how we are born as well as parental anxieties and expectations. In Layla's case, as she got older it was simply painful to take her to social activities because she was such a timid child. Unfortunately, however, this meant that she had little opportunity to experience being in social groups, to learn to enjoy them, and to develop skills to cope with them.

## So, what has made my child so anxious?

The information presented in the chapters so far shows that there is clearly no straightforward answer to this question. Various factors influence children's fears and worries, and each of these factors can influence the others. If your child has developed fears and worries, the most important question now, however, is not what has caused these fears and worries but what is keeping them going. One way to think about this is like a car stuck in the mud – once the car is stuck we need to focus on how to get the car unstuck, rather than what road the car took that led to them getting stuck in the first place. This is the focus of the next chapter.

**Key points**

- Anxiety often runs in families

- Anxiety is caused by a whole range of factors

- Children who are prone to fears and worries may be particularly influenced by, for example, difficult life events or other people's reactions

- It is normal for parents/carers to want to protect their children, but this needs to be balanced against giving them opportunities to 'have a go'

# 5

# What keeps children's fears and worries going?

### Sarah

*Sarah doesn't actually come across spiders very often, as she makes one of us go into her room if she thinks there might be one so that we can check and get rid of any we find. If she does ever see a spider she just gets away as quickly as she can. She just has this idea that the spider is going to crawl up her arm. I think that's pretty unlikely really and I've told her that I'm sure the spider is more scared of her than she is of it, but because she just clears off she never gets to see that the spiders are harmless.*

## Vicious cycles

Fears and worries are all about vicious cycles. In Chapter 1 we described the three main aspects of anxiety: (i) expecting that something 'bad' might happen; (ii) bodily changes; and (iii) avoidance and safety-seeking behaviour. These are the key components that make up anxiety itself, but they also act to keep each other going. For example, as shown in Figure 5.1 when Sarah comes across a spider, her first thought is 'It is going to crawl up my arm and I will freak out', and her heart starts to beat quickly, giving her more evidence that something bad is going to happen. Not surprisingly she tries to get away. 'Thank goodness,' she thinks, 'it's lucky I got away or that spider would have crawled up my arm.' The next time she comes across a spider the same thing happens again.

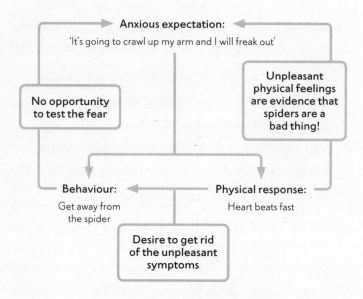

Figure 5.1 Trigger: Sarah sees a spider

## Anxious expectations revisited

When people have fears or worries they are likely to have one or both of two common types of thought. The first are thoughts to do with threat: when people experience anxiety they often *overestimate* how likely it is that something bad is going to happen. For example, they think that they will definitely do badly in a test. Second are thoughts about coping: people who are highly anxious tend to *underestimate* their ability to cope with what might happen. That is, they expect that they will not be able to cope. For example, if they struggle in a test, they predict they will panic, give up and start crying.

Thinking in these ways can get in the way of new learning as we then notice things that are going on around us that fit in with our beliefs, and either fail to notice or disregard things that don't fit with our beliefs. We all have a natural tendency to filter new information in this way – but the problem is that it can keep unhelpful beliefs going and stop us from learning new things. For example, imagine a man who has developed a firm belief that people who wear hats when they drive are terrible drivers. Whenever he notices anyone wearing a hat while driving he is on the lookout for any mistake that they might make. If he doesn't see the person make a mistake he discounts this bit of evidence and concludes that they must have been concentrating particularly hard at that time, but that they are no doubt a terrible driver most of the time. Other drivers may well make mistakes, too, but he is less likely to notice them, as he is not really paying particular attention to what they do.

Fears work in exactly the same way. Our attention is firmly focused on noticing and remembering things that confirm the fear, and away from things that do not fit with the fear. If we do see examples that run contrary to our fearful beliefs, we may not learn anything new from it because we come up with reasons why that evidence doesn't count.

Recent research has suggested that many preadolescent children tend to see the world in a threatening way (for example, expecting animals to be dangerous) but this appears to reduce as children get older. What seems to be particularly important in determining whether children feel anxious or not are their thoughts about being able to cope. Recent research also suggests that developing a view of oneself as someone who can cope with challenges may be particularly important for children to recover from difficulties with anxiety.

## Bodily changes revisited

When we consider the anxious thoughts that Muhammed and Layla are having in the previous examples it is not at all surprising that they are feeling fear and experiencing physical symptoms of fear, such as a racing heart, sweaty palms and an unsettled stomach (feeling sick, tummy ache). These kinds of symptoms can be uncomfortable and alarming, and may lead to even more anxiety. If a child interprets the physical changes as (i) evidence that something bad is happening; (ii) a sign that something is seriously wrong with his or her body; or (iii) too uncomfortable to bear, then he or she is likely to feel even more fearful and will want to stay away from any situations that could bring on this kind of reaction. In other words, the child starts to fear the bodily symptoms of fear.

Bodily changes may also increase fears and worries by affecting a child's performance. In Layla's case, for example, shaking, sweating and having a lump in her throat will make it difficult to speak up in front of other people. Being aware of this may make her even less confident about asking a question; then, when the time comes, she will feel even more worried and experience even more physical symptoms. Layla's fear of not being able to give a presentation was likely to bring about what she most feared: that is, not being able to speak in front of the class.

Figure 5.2 Trigger: Layla is asked to speak in front of her class

## *Anxious behaviour revisited*

When we consider not only the anxious thoughts that Layla and Muhammed were having but also the uncomfortable physical sensations that they experienced, it is very understandable why they are behaving the way that they are.

### AVOIDANCE

A natural reaction to a threat is to get away from it. In the short term this is sometimes a sensible solution. However, by not facing the feared situation a person never gets to

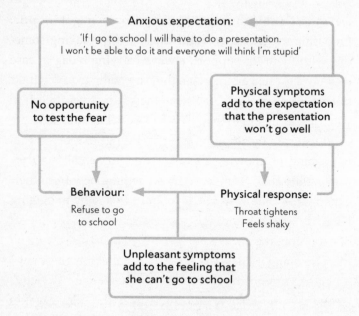

Figure 5.3 Trigger: Layla is due to give a presentation in school

discover whether it really is as bad as they fear or learns how to cope with it. By staying home from school, Layla didn't get to see that it was quite normal to be nervous about giving presentations. Many of her classmates also showed signs of fear, but this seemed to be understood by the classmates rather than laughed at. She also didn't get a chance to practise and become good at standing up and speaking in front of her peers.

## SAFETY-SEEKING BEHAVIOURS

As well as more obvious avoidance behaviours, children may do things in a very particular way that allows them to feel safe. These 'safety-seeking behaviours' might include: preparing meticulously in advance, always having some- one with them for support, always carrying a bag in case they are sick, rehearsing what they are going to say in their mind before speaking, or letting their hair cover their face when speaking up. In their mind, these behaviours help the child feel safe by stopping (or preventing) the 'bad thing' happening or allowing them to cope. In actual fact they prevent the child from learning something new from their experiences. One way to think about this is by imagining a person who is standing in their garden throwing pieces of paper into the air. When their neighbour asks them why they are doing it, they answer, 'To keep the dragons away'. 'But there are no dragons,' says the neighbour, 'Exactly,' they reply'. In other words, sometimes the things we do to keep ourselves safe stop us from learning that we are already safe.

We can see this happen in Ben's example in Figure 5.4, after going upstairs to get his jumper, he concludes that 'it was fine [but only] because my brother was with me.'

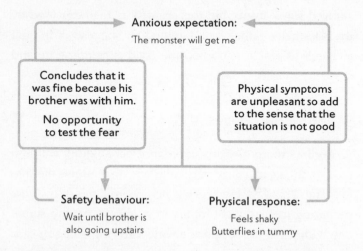

Figure 5.4 Trigger: Ben needs to get a jumper from upstairs

## REASSURANCE-SEEKING

Like avoidance, getting reassurance from someone else (usually an adult) may make the child feel better right at that moment. If a child is constantly seeking reassurance, however, then it shows that she has not used this information to change or update her 'fear belief' but has used it for only short-term relief. Imagine a child who constantly asks their parent whether they are going to be OK before going out the house. The child may eventually leave the house, but the next time may need the same reassurance rather than having the skills and confidence to manage their anxiety themselves. In other words, reassurance can lead to greater dependence on more reassurance in the future. Yet another vicious cycle. Another example of this is shown for Ben below.

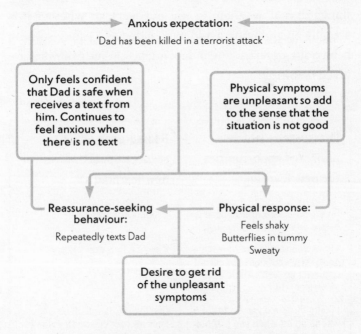

Figure 5.5 Trigger: Ben's dad is late home from work

At times, providing children with reassurance can be helpful, and indeed an important part of being a parent and encouraging and supporting your child to do something they haven't tried before. So, parents often ask us when giving reassurance is and isn't OK. A helpful way to think about this is to ask yourself whether your reassurance-giving is helping your child to have a go at new things that allow them to test out fears, or whether it is actually encouraging avoidance, acting as a safety-seeking behaviour, or restricting independence. Some examples are given below.

| Reassurance which promotes opportunities for new learning: | Reassurance which reduces opportunities for new learning: |
|---|---|
| Go on, have a go, you've done it before and it went really well. | It's OK, Mummy's here. |
| I think you should see how it goes. I feel confident but even if it doesn't go well we will have an idea of what to work on next. | It will be fine, don't worry! |
| I really think you can do this. I was so proud when you asked a question in class last week. | Don't worry, it will all be OK. I'm sure your classmates won't laugh, and the teacher is bound to be really nice. |

## How other people respond

The way that other people respond to a child can clearly make a difference to these vicious cycles. In the previous chapter we discussed how anxiety can develop in children in part because they may have learnt anxious feelings and behaviours from other people around them. In Chapter 4 we specifically talked about (i) learning by example; (ii) learning from other people's reactions to the child; and (iii) having limited opportunities to face fears and develop skills. While we may be able to 'get away with' these behaviours with a less-anxious child, more-anxious children are likely to be more tuned into our reactions, so if you or other people (other carers, siblings, teachers and so on) are still responding to your child in any of these ways then this may also be helping to *keep the fears and worries going*.

An example of this is given in Figure 5.6. Given her frequent experience of Layla becoming distressed about going to school, we can understand her Mum's reaction. As Layla was starting to get ready for school her mum felt nervous based on her worry that Layla would get herself in a state. She kept asking Layla if she was OK, which, unfortunately, in combination with her visible nervousness reinforced the message for Layla that there might be reason to think that things might not be OK! As we can see, when it was time to go in to school, Layla became extremely anxious, driven by her general fear that things were going to go badly in some way, and particularly that she would do something that people would think was stupid and they would laugh at her. She felt her throat tighten and she felt shaky. Both of these sets of symptoms were very unpleasant and added to her concern that she was going to look silly in front of others, as they would notice these symptoms. Understandably, Layla refused to go in to school – but, by not going in, Layla was not able to test out her fears, get support and find ways to manage. In turn, Layla's response was evidence for her mum's anxious expectations.

To recap, if people around a child are showing signs of fear and responding to these with avoidance, then a child (particularly a sensitive child who may be on the lookout for information that fits with their 'fear belief') is likely to learn that the particular object or situation presents a threat and that the best way to respond is by avoiding it. Equally, if carers are responding to a child's attempts at facing fear with particular concern and instead try to encourage the child to keep away from fears, this may also give the child the message that there is something to fear or that they will be unable to cope. This could again make the child more likely to try to avoid challenging situations. Finally, if a child does not get the opportunities to face fears then they will not get the information they need to test out fear beliefs and develop the skills needed to become able to deal with challenges independently.

Now we have talked about what might be maintaining your child's anxiety, have a go at filling in the worksheet on page 52. Think about a recent situation that your child has struggled with. See if you can figure out what might be keeping these sorts of fears going. If you feel that the

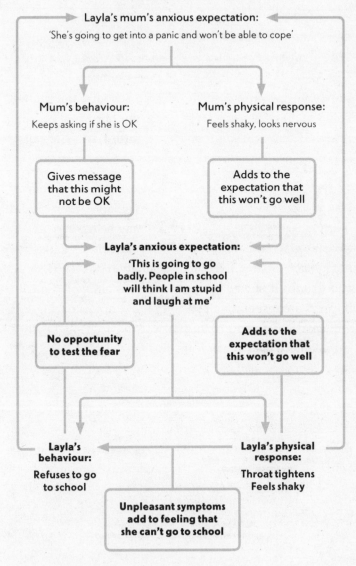

Figure 5.6 Trigger: Layla is getting ready for school in the morning

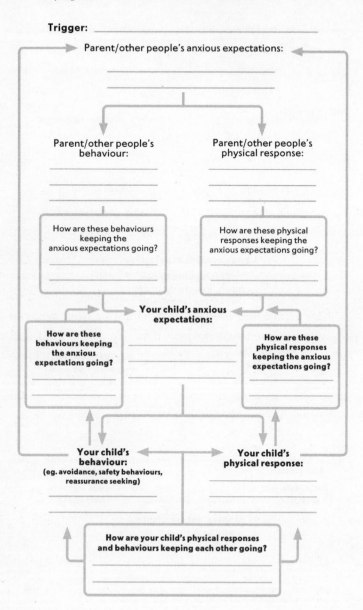

Figure 5.7

reactions of other people around the child are also important, complete the top section too. If you struggle to do
this keep reading through the following chapters and then
come back to this before you make a start on working with
your child.

## Breaking the cycles

The central aim of the next section of this book is to help
you and your child to break the cycles that are keeping
their fears and worries going. Specifically, we will be guid-
ing you through ways to work out what your child needs
to learn, and to work with your child to help them put their
anxious expectations to the test. As we have described
in this chapter and the last, as a parent or carer you can
have a big influence on how your child learns to think and
behave. Throughout the next chapters we will be helping
you to pay attention to how you and other important people in your child's life are responding to their anxieties and
supporting them to develop a new approach to life.

---

**Key points**

- Children who have problems with anxiety often expect
  something bad to happen and that they won't be able
  to cope

- Anxious expectations can keep anxiety going

- Children sometimes fear bodily sensations

- Avoidance can stop children from challenging their anxious expectations

- Reassurance and anxious reactions from others can keep child anxiety problems going

# PART II

◇◇◇◇◇◇◇◇◇◇◇◇

## Helping Your Child Overcome Fears and Worries

# 6

# How to use this book

## A guide to Part Two

Many children experience difficulties with fears and worries at some time or other, and very often families are able to overcome the problems fairly quickly and easily. For some children the fear seems to just be 'a phase'. For others, the fear may exist but without causing any particular problems for the child or family: they are not having to avoid doing anything they would like to be doing and the child is not bothered by the presence of the fear (for example, a child who is fearful of snakes but rarely comes into contact with them). For others, however, the fears or worries may go on longer or cause more disruption to the child's or family members' lives. The child may frequently be distressed and avoid doing things because of the fear. Members of the family may be working so hard to minimise the child's distress that they are unable to get on with what they would like to be doing. In this situation many families will require professional support, and it is important that they seek this help and receive it.

Many families could, however, if they knew how, over-come these difficulties themselves. This book is designed to help families who are prepared to have a go at helping their child overcome these fears and worries themselves but are unsure where to begin.

## Before you start

### Why change?

It would be understandable if you had some mixed feelings about changing things in your child's, and your own, life. Looking after an anxious child can be distressing in itself, and often exhausting, and it is likely that it has taken a great effort on your part to get by as well as you have and to keep your child's distress to a minimum. We are sure that you will have anticipated that inevitably this programme is going to involve your child facing their fears. As we said before, the evolutionary urge to protect your child is very strong, and the thought of encouraging your child to start doing things that might initially involve them experiencing some anxiety and distress can be hard to imagine. You are likely to have tried this before and may have found that this caused more upset than seemed worthwhile. Maybe, you are thinking, you should just carry on as you are? Maybe he or she will grow out of it? Maybe trying to do something about the situation will just make things worse? These are all under-standable reactions to the thought of changing things. Our hunch is that if you are reading this book then things have got to a point where your child's fears or worries are getting in the way to some extent. In many cases, children do not grow out of their anxiety problems (although the focus of the anxiety may change). However, there is good research to show that children are likely to overcome anxiety successfully if the principles in this book are followed.

## When to change?

It is important to be aware that to be able to apply the principles in this book consistently and regularly will require you to make this a priority for the next couple of months. If you are about to go on holiday for two weeks, or you are approaching a major deadline at work, you may not be able to commit yourself sufficiently to this programme straight away. Similarly, if your child is about to go away on a school trip, you don't want to make a start that can't be followed up for over a week. In these circumstances, it would be best to postpone starting the programme until you are in a position to make this your number-one priority.

Having said that, there may always seem to be one reason or another to postpone getting started, but at some stage you are going to have to start. So, unless there is a serious reason for not doing so (like those given above), you should set yourself a start date for some time soon. What we would suggest is that you get started now by reading through this entire section within the next week or so. You will then have a clear idea of what is going to be involved in order to set your date for getting started with your child.

## What to change?

Some children will experience just one very specific fear, such as dogs, but the majority of children we see experience anxiety about a number of different things. If your child has just one clear fear then it will not be a problem for you in deciding what to focus on. If, however, your child seems to worry about all kinds of things, you will need to decide early on what you are going to make your initial focus. It is very important that you do choose *one* particular fear or worry to focus upon. This keeps things simpler for you and your child, and the gains that are made will be clear and obvious to you both. You may feel that by picking one fear you are dealing with just 'the tip of the iceberg', but this need not put you off, for two reasons. First, skills will be learned and practised by you and your child. It will then be easier to apply them to other fears (one by one). Second, having success at overcoming one fear will teach your child some valuable lessons, which will have knock-on effects for other fears: (i) that fears can be overcome; and (ii) that she or he is capable of overcoming them. We will help you think further about what to focus on in Chapter 7.

# About the self-help programme

The following chapters introduce you to the most important part of the programme: the steps you can use to overcome your child's fears and worries. These follow the basic elements of cognitive behavioural therapy (CBT) for children with anxiety problems. CBT refers to treatment based on the idea that how we think about things is associated with how we behave and how we feel. Therefore, by changing how we think about our fears, and how we act because of them, we can change how we feel about them. This type of therapy is widely used with adults and children and has, in the last decade, become a treatment of choice for many emotional problems, particularly anxiety difficulties. A number of treatment studies have shown that where the principles described in this book are followed consistently, children benefit considerably.

## The five steps

The five main principles are shown in the box on page 62. These principles can also be treated as steps, as they follow each other in the order that is given. We will give more information on each step throughout the next chapters.

In addition to the five steps shown in the box, there are three further chapters at the end of this part of the book.

Chapter 12 provides guidelines on what you can do if your child is 'a worrier'. By this we mean someone who thinks about different worries over and over again and finds it hard to control these worries; this might be causing your child to become easily distressed, making them tense, making it hard for them to sleep or perhaps causing problems with concentration at school. If this does apply to your child then we would recommend applying these principles throughout the whole course of your programme (that is, while you are working through the five steps).

Chapter 14 concerns managing your own anxiety. It's clearly not always the case, but many parents who we work with also experience difficulties with anxiety themselves. Parents who also experience difficulties with anxiety may face some particular challenges in helping their child to overcome fears and worries. If you feel this may apply to you, we would encourage you to read Chapter 14 before you get started.

Many children who exhibit high levels of anxiety and worry also experience unpleasant, physical symptoms. Chapter 13 gives some specific guidance on helping children to deal with those unpleasant bodily reactions. Again, if this applies to your child do read Chapter 13 before getting started.

### Step 1 Setting goals

Being clear about what you want to achieve

### Step 2 Working out what your child needs to learn

Asking the right questions (in the right way) to understand what your child is thinking

### Step 3 Encouraging independence and 'having a go'

Using praise and rewards and other strategies to encourage brave behaviour

### Step 4 Developing a step-by-step plan with your child

Helping your child to make a plan for gradually facing his or her fears to test out anxious predictions

### Step 5 Problem-solving

Helping your child to become an independent problem-solver

## *Addressing particular needs*

In Part Three, additional techniques are described that may or may not apply to you and your child, depending on the nature of your child's fears. These concern sleep problems, difficult behaviour and school problems. We have also included a chapter aimed at teachers or other school staff that can be copied and passed on to people that work with your child at school if this would be useful.

The main sections of this book use case examples and material that will be relevant to children of primary school age (5 to 12 years). Two chapters in Part Three are, however, devoted to discussing what you will need to take into account if your child is at the younger or older end of this age group. We would recommend that you read Chapter 16 if your child is 7 years of age or younger, or Chapter 17 if your child is about 11 years or older. We suggest you read one of those chapters before you get started so you can apply the principles throughout the whole course of your programme.

## Getting the most out of this book

Throughout this programme the emphasis is on you helping your child to overcome his or her anxieties. Rather than solving problems for your child or reassuring him or her that everything will be fine, your role will be to act as both coach and cheerleader. You will be in charge of helping your child to work out what to do for themselves and then cheering on their progress. At the end of the day it will be your child who has to deal with problems; you cannot guarantee that you'll always be there when a problem arises, so it is essential that your child is learning, with help from you, how to deal with fears and worries on their own. Nonetheless, it is possible that you see your child's fears and worries as a bigger problem than your child does. For example, if a child feels nervous about attending school he or she may not think that the answer is to overcome this fear and go to school. Instead, he or she may think that the best thing to do is simply not go to school. Although you need to work with and guide your child, it is also your responsibility to take the lead, encourage, motivate and set a good example to your child. Throughout this section we will consider ways of encouraging your child to get involved. There are also additional tips in Chapter 17 for increasing motivation while using this book with older children and adolescents.

As you can see from the table of steps on pages 62–3, some of the steps involve asking your child questions to help him or her work things out for themselves. To do this successfully you need to be asking the right questions. This is not always easy, but we will help you. It is essential that the questions are asked in a way that shows your child you are taking his or her worries seriously – that you are not making fun or being critical. This can be difficult at times, particularly if you are feeling frustrated by your child's behaviour. For your child to work with you, you need to show that you understand and accept what your child is worried about. However, you also need to communicate that you recognise that this worry is getting in the way and so something needs to be done about it.

Whilst the worries themselves need to be taken seriously, in working together to overcome them you can enjoy yourselves. Take every opportunity to have fun and be creative. If the whole programme is heavy and emotional your child is not going to want to be involved, so try to keep the mood light where you can!

## Keeping written records

Throughout the book we ask you to keep records of the work that you do with your child. Some parents like to work through these with their children; others sit down later and complete them. Either way please do put pen to paper and complete them, for two reasons. First, writing things down helps learning and remembering. Second, this allows you to look back later to see where you had got to. Often parents will feel as if things have been moving slowly or even backwards, but then when they actually look at their written records they see that a lot of progress has been made. It is easy to feel that what is happening right now has been happening for ever, but this is generally not the case. (As with all the charts we use in the book, not all of the questions will be relevant to your particular situation; just answer those that apply to your own or your child's experiences.)

## You don't need to go it alone

We often work with single parents who put this programme into practice very successfully on their own. There is no doubt, however, that it will be easier to work through the programme with your child if you have help from others around you. This may be a partner, parent, older child, a friend or your child's teacher. The more people there are around your child following the same principles, the easier it will be for your child to learn how to overcome fears and worries. Equally, working with another adult is likely to motivate you and keep you going at times when it feels like a struggle. Sometimes the strategies that we suggest may be tricky. In particular it can be difficult to stick to asking questions rather than giving your child reassurance or trying to solve problems for him or her. You may feel embarrassed at first, but having a practice run at these conversations with another adult will help prepare you for talking through these things with your child. Your 'partner' can help you work out which questions worked well, whether the tone was right and whether your child would feel understood and taken seriously.

## Keeping it going

The final chapter in this section is all about keeping your child's progress going. We hope that having read all the way through this book you will feel charged up and ready to start tackling your child's difficulties. It is just as likely that this feeling will plummet when you hit your first hurdle. You may feel that you have failed, that you're not doing it properly and that your child will never recover. It is really important to stress that if overcoming your child's problems were easy, you would have done it long ago. You must be prepared for the fact that there *will* be setbacks – times when your child does not make as much progress as you had hoped, or even seems to go backwards. Additionally, your child has been in a pattern of thinking, behaving and feeling a certain way for some time – and this is not likely to change overnight. However, if you follow the principles described here you will be helping your child to take control of these fears or worries, and you will almost certainly make progress.

So now it is time to take your first step and read what is involved in helping your child overcome his or her fears and worries.

# 7

# Step 1: What are your goals?

Before you start to work with your child on their anxiety problems, it is important to think about where you both want to get to and what you want your child to achieve. Setting clear goals will help you to keep on track and ensure you are focusing on the things that are most important to you and your child. It also means you can easily track how your child is getting on, and how much progress they have made, and will hopefully give you and your child a clear way to see that things are getting better.

In this chapter, we help you to come up with some clear, specific goals for the short, medium and long term, and also help you to decide what to focus on first. Where possible, it will be best to set goals *with* your child, asking your child questions and letting them take the lead. If your child is motivated to achieve the goal this will make your job a lot easier. Try to keep the conversation relaxed and positive, focusing on what your child would like to be able to do that they cannot do or find difficult to do now. However, sometimes children do not want to even think about goals as they know it will mean having to face fears that they would rather avoid. If this is the case, you will need to take the lead in setting goals for your child. If you need to take this approach we recommend keeping the goals very modest at first, so your child gets a positive experience of having a go, despite not wanting to, which will encourage them to work with you to set and work towards other, more ambitious, goals in the future.

## How to identify goals

It is worth keeping two main ideas in mind when setting goals:

### 1. Focus on the positive

It is often easy to think about what you *don't* want your child to be doing or feeling (e.g. I don't want my child to feel so anxious when they go to school) but this type of goal doesn't tell you or your child what they *could* be working towards and can be difficult to measure. In contrast, things become much simpler if you can specify what you would like your child to be doing. For example, Sarah's mum wanted her not to scream and run away when she sees a spider. When she considered what she wanted Sarah to do, she decided the goal would be for Sarah to ask for her parents to remove a spider from her room calmly while she watched.

### 2. Focus on behaviours

It is also much easier to observe and measure what your

child *does* rather than how they feel. For this reason, set goals that describe what your child will be able to do once they have overcome their current difficulties with anxiety. Muhammed's mum and dad wanted Muhammed not to be scared when he went upstairs. When they thought about what they wanted Muhammed to do rather than feel, they decided their goal would be for him to be able to play upstairs alone for at least half an hour.

There are some questions you can ask yourself to start to think about what the goals might be. These will help you to identify what you want to work on.

---

*Questions to help you to identify your goals*

If your child were no longer anxious, what would he be doing that he isn't doing at the moment?

What would your child be doing differently if she didn't have a problem with anxiety?

What changes would you notice?

What would you like your child to do that they are not doing currently?

What is your child missing out on due to their anxiety?

What would your child need to do, for you to think they have overcome their difficulties with anxiety?

---

We would recommend that you have between one and three goals to start with, focusing on the things that would really make a difference to your child's life. You will then want to work on these one at a time.

So how do you decide which goals to choose? Here are some questions that will help you to decide:

*1. What would make the biggest difference to my child's life?*

This is what Layla's mum thought: 'If Layla could talk to her friends at school and invite them over, it would make a big difference to her school and home life and improve her general mood, whereas if Layla could sit in the school canteen at lunchtime, it would make a small difference to her school and home life. So, we decided that one of our goals is for Layla to invite her friends over.'

*2. If we got rid of one anxiety problem, would others go away?*

For example, if your child was less worried about how they were getting on at school, would they be happier separating from you in the mornings?

*3. Will one anxiety problem get in the way of tackling another one?*

In Muhammed's case, his parents reported: 'It would be very difficult for Muhammed to play with his friends at a party if he is still worried about separating from me. So, we decided that we needed to work on separation first.'

If you are still left with more than one goal on your list,

*4. Which goal would be the easiest to achieve?*

Sometimes starting with the easiest goal is sensible, as it gives you all a sense of achievement and confidence to tackler the bigger goals.

## Are your goals SMART?

Once you have a good idea of what sorts of things you would like your child to be doing (that they are not doing at the moment), and what you would like to work on first, the next step is to make sure that your goal or goals are SMART. SMART goals are Specific, Measurable, Achievable, Realistic, and have a realistic Time frame.

---

**SMART Goals**

*Is it Specific?*

Is it clear exactly what my child has to do?

*Is it Measurable?*

Can I easily measure whether and to what extent my child has done this, or will I easily know when it has been done?

*Is it Achievable?*

Can my child actually achieve this, is there anything that might get in the way?

*Is it Realistic?*

Is this a realistic goal for my child, can they do this?

*Is the Time frame appropriate?*

Can my child achieve this in a sensible amount of time (we would recommend aiming for a goal that can be achieved in a month or two at the most)?

Have a look at the table below for some examples that might help you to turn general goals into SMART goals.

| General goal | Question | Specific goal |
|---|---|---|
| To be more confident in social situations | If she were more confident in social situations what would she be doing? | To invite a friend to our house for tea |
| To worry less | If he were worrying less what would he be doing? | To go to bed without calling us to come up after we have said goodnight |
| To be relaxed around dogs | If she were relaxed around dogs what would she be able to do? | To go to the park and play with her friends for an hour while people are walking their dogs |
| To be less anxious | If he was less anxious what would he be able to do? | To play at his grandparents' house for 2 hours |

# Start small!

It is likely that you may want to address a big issue all at once (e.g. *'I want my child to be in school full-time'*; *'I want my child to go on the school residential trip next month'*), but we would recommend starting with small, SMART goals so that your targets are not overwhelming and so that you can quickly see progress. Once your child has achieved these, you can move on to other, more ambitious goals. One way of doing this is to agree some short-, medium- and long-term goals. For example, a short-term goal is something you would like to achieve over the next 2–4 weeks. A long-term goal might take you 6 months to achieve. If you do this, you won't lose sight of what you want your child to achieve in the end, but you will still be 'starting small'.

---

**Examples of short-, medium- and long-term goals**

*Layla's goals*

| | |
|---|---|
| Short: | To ask the teacher a question at breaktime |
| Medium: | To ask the teacher a question in front of the class |
| Long: | To read out loud in front of the school in assembly |

*Sarah's goals*

| | |
|---|---|
| Short: | To be able to watch calmly while her parents remove a spider from her room |
| Medium: | To be able to go in the loft, garage and shed |
| Long: | To hold a live spider in her hand |

**Muhammed's goals**

Short:       To be able to stay in bed after parents
             say goodnight (parents can still check in
             regularly)

Medium:      To be able to settle to sleep by himself

Long:        To be able to sleep on his own all night for
             a week

**Ben's goals**

Short:       To be able to play on the computer
             upstairs for ½ hour by himself

Medium:      To be able to spend up to an hour upstairs
             and go up and down stairs when he needs
             to without having someone with him

Long:        To be able to sleep in his room alone

Using the tips above, now think about and write down the goals that you and your child will work on (choose between 1 and 3 and put them in order of priority i.e. which one do you want to work on 1st, 2nd and 3rd).

You will then need to decide if you are going to help your child to aim for the short-, medium- or long-term goal from the start. Think about which one will be most motivating for your child. Some children prefer to look at the bigger picture and may be frustrated by only aiming for a short-term goal. However, other children may feel overwhelmed by a long-term goal and this may put them off completely. Talk to your child about which goal they would like to aim for.

|  | Short-term | Medium-term | Long-term |
|---|---|---|---|
| Goal 1 |  |  |  |
| Goal 2 |  |  |  |
| Goal 3 |  |  |  |

## Reviewing Progress

It is important to review your goals on a regular basis. This will help you to keep focused and to identify the progress you and your child have made. Often doing this weekly can be a helpful time frame for review. Parents are often really surprised when they review their child's progress as they have sometimes forgotten how difficult things were when they first started the programme (*'Wow, I forgot that x was so anxious about dogs that we couldn't even walk down the street!'*) or may not have realised how much progress their child has made (*'We have nearly achieved our first goal, I really didn't think that was possible when we started out!'*). We would suggest you rate progress on all your goals, even though you are likely to only be focusing on one at a time. We have found that sometimes children make progress with other goals even when they are not the main focus.

In order to review each of your goals use the following 0–10 scale.

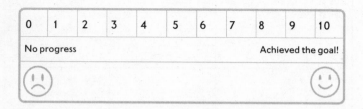

(0 = no progress, 10 = achieved the goal).

On the pages 79–84 you will find a set of these scales. Mark dates by each one at weekly intervals and make yourself a note to come back to this page and rate your progress towards your goals once a week from when you start the programme. It is sometimes helpful not only to make your own rating but to also ask your child, your partner, other relatives and friends, for their rating too. Other people will sometimes spot progress that you might have missed, especially if you are focused on a longer-term goal (e.g. '*I really need to get my child back into school full-time*'). We will keep asking you to rate your child's progress throughout the book.

**Monitoring progress**

GOAL 1 _____

(Are you using the short-, medium- or long-term goal? Make sure it's SMART!)

**Start date:** _____

Rating:

| 0 | 1 | 2 | 3 | 4 | 5 | 6 | 7 | 8 | 9 | 10 |
|---|---|---|---|---|---|---|---|---|---|----|
| No progress | | | | | | | | | Achieved the goal! | |

(0 = no progress, 10 = achieved the goal).

**End of week 1; Date:** _____

Rating:

| 0 | 1 | 2 | 3 | 4 | 5 | 6 | 7 | 8 | 9 | 10 |
|---|---|---|---|---|---|---|---|---|---|----|

No progress                                                    Achieved the goal!

(0 = no progress, 10 = achieved the goal).

**End of week 2; Date:** _____

Rating:

| 0 | 1 | 2 | 3 | 4 | 5 | 6 | 7 | 8 | 9 | 10 |
|---|---|---|---|---|---|---|---|---|---|----|

No progress                                                    Achieved the goal!

(0 = no progress, 10 = achieved the goal).

**End of week 3; Date:** _____

Rating:

| 0 | 1 | 2 | 3 | 4 | 5 | 6 | 7 | 8 | 9 | 10 |
|---|---|---|---|---|---|---|---|---|---|----|

No progress                                    Achieved the goal!

(0 = no progress, 10 = achieved the goal).

**End of week 4; Date:** _____

Rating:

| 0 | 1 | 2 | 3 | 4 | 5 | 6 | 7 | 8 | 9 | 10 |
|---|---|---|---|---|---|---|---|---|---|----|

No progress                                    Achieved the goal!

(0 = no progress, 10 = achieved the goal).

**End of week 5; Date:** _____

Rating:

| 0 | 1 | 2 | 3 | 4 | 5 | 6 | 7 | 8 | 9 | 10 |
|---|---|---|---|---|---|---|---|---|---|----|

No progress                                        Achieved the goal!

(0 = no progress, 10 = achieved the goal).

**End of week 6; Date:** _____

Rating:

| 0 | 1 | 2 | 3 | 4 | 5 | 6 | 7 | 8 | 9 | 10 |
|---|---|---|---|---|---|---|---|---|---|----|

No progress                                        Achieved the goal!

(0 = no progress, 10 = achieved the goal).

**End of week 7; Date:** _____

Rating:

| 0 | 1 | 2 | 3 | 4 | 5 | 6 | 7 | 8 | 9 | 10 |
|---|---|---|---|---|---|---|---|---|---|---|

No progress                                    Achieved the goal!

(0 = no progress, 10 = achieved the goal).

**End of week 8; Date:** _____

Rating:

| 0 | 1 | 2 | 3 | 4 | 5 | 6 | 7 | 8 | 9 | 10 |
|---|---|---|---|---|---|---|---|---|---|---|

No progress                                    Achieved the goal!

(0 = no progress, 10 = achieved the goal).

**End of week 9; Date:** _____

Rating:

| 0 | 1 | 2 | 3 | 4 | 5 | 6 | 7 | 8 | 9 | 10 |
|---|---|---|---|---|---|---|---|---|---|----|

No progress                                        Achieved the goal!

(0 = no progress, 10 = achieved the goal).

**End of week 10; Date:** _____

Rating:

| 0 | 1 | 2 | 3 | 4 | 5 | 6 | 7 | 8 | 9 | 10 |
|---|---|---|---|---|---|---|---|---|---|----|

No progress                                        Achieved the goal!

(0 = no progress, 10 = achieved the goal).

*THEN REPEAT STAGES FOR GOALS 2 AND 3*

# Troubleshooting

## I am struggling to set goals with my child

There are a number of different reasons it can be hard to agree SMART goals with your child. Below are some common difficulties and suggestions about how to overcome these:

### 1. My child is not interested in overcoming their anxieties

If this is the case, start by setting your own goals for your child and try to work on these using the strategies outlined later in the book. If you do this, start with very modest goals so that your child gets a positive experience of setting and attempting goals. This may, then, encourage them to work with you in setting the next set of goals. Chapter 9 talks about how you can motivate your child using praise and rewards for tackling their anxiety problems.

### 2. My child's goals are different to mine (or my partner's goals are different to mine)

It can be tricky if you and either your child or partner would like to work on different goals. As we have said, you can have more than one goal, but it is helpful to prioritise what you will work on first rather than trying to tackle everything at once.

In general, we recommend prioritising your child's goals as they are likely to be more motivated to work on something that is important to them. However, occasionally your goals will need to override your child's goals, e.g. if they are not attending school, you may need to address this as soon as possible even if your child does not want to. In this situation it can be helpful to have two goals, one that you have set and one that your child has set, and agree to work on these both alongside each other with equal enthusiasm.

### 3. *My child has so many anxieties, I don't know where to start*

Take another look at the four questions on page 72 to try to help you decide where to start. If you are still struggling, we would suggest you start with something easy – that way you and your child will notice good progress quickly, which will enable you to move onto more challenging goals. So, focus on a short-term goal to start with and then move on to your medium- and long-term goals when you have achieved this.

### 4. *My child tends to worry about things, but s/he doesn't avoid particular situations or things, so it is hard to have goals focused on behaviour*

This is a tricky one – often children with generalised anxiety say that their goal is to 'worry less'. We would suggest asking yourself or your child: What would they be doing if they worried less, that they don't do at the moment? Would they be settling to sleep more quickly or not calling out at night? Would they play with their friends more at playtime rather than sitting by themselves worrying? Would they be completing their homework within half an hour, rather than spending hours on a single piece of work to ensure it is absolutely perfect?

## Key points

- Set goals before you start the programme; this will help you to stay on track and to monitor your child's progress

- Make sure your goals are SMART

- Agree short-, medium- and long-term goals

- Identify a maximum of three goals and decide which one to work on first

- Review your goals regularly to give you a sense of achievement, and ask others to rate them, too

# 8

# Step 2: What does your child need to learn?

The next step is to try to identify *what your child needs to learn* in order to put their anxious expectations to the test and to achieve their goals. This will help you to decide how to use the strategies described in this book, to help your child overcome their difficulties with anxiety. Figuring out what your child needs to learn is probably the most important of the steps, so please take your time and don't rush to complete this. What children need to learn to overcome particular problems with anxiety can vary widely. The key thing to remember throughout this step is to be *curious*! Keep an open mind. There are no right or wrong answers. You simply need to ask questions, listen to what your child says, observe their behaviour and take note.

If your child is young (eight years of age or younger) or appears to struggle with what you are trying to do then you may find Chapter 16 helpful, as this focuses specifically on making the strategies in this book more suitable for younger children.

# What are my child's anxious expectations?

Anxious children often seem to be 'on the lookout' for threat and to 'jump to conclusions' about threat. If there is some uncertainty about what is going on they may expect something bad will happen. In some of our studies we haven't necessarily found that children who have difficulties with anxiety think in a more threat-focused way than children who don't have these difficulties, but they do seem to feel less able to deal with dangers that might be thrown at them and are more likely to try to stay away from these situations or become more distressed compared to other children.

It is important to get a good idea of what your child's fears or worries are and understand what they expect to happen in order to help you work out what they need to learn so that they can overcome these difficulties. This section will help you to do this.

Some children are great at talking about their worries or anxious thoughts; some talk about them all the time! However, for some children it is really hard to talk about them; they may not always even have a clear idea of what they are worried about. In the next section, we give you lots of tips and hints to help you figure this out.

## Asking questions – being curious

The box below gives some examples of questions you can ask to help your child tell you what it is that worries them or what they are afraid of. Use these questions when you spot signs that your child is feeling anxious.

Clearly, there is nothing very clever or magical about these questions. However, they all start with 'What' or 'Why'. These are called 'open' questions. Compare these to what are called 'closed' questions – for example: 'Do you worry that you will get hurt?', 'Are you worried that the dog will bite you?' Your child can just give you a yes or no answer to closed questions, which may not help you very much as you try to get a better understanding of what he or she is thinking. Open questions, on the other hand, do not limit the response in this way, and you are likely to get a lot more helpful information. We would recommend you try to stick to open questions as much as possible.

### Understanding anxious expectations

*Example questions to ask:*

'Why are you feeling worried?'

'What is frightening you?'

'What do you think will happen?'

'What is the worst thing that might happen?'

'What is it about [this situation] that is making you worried?'

# Getting the best results

*How* you ask your child about their worries, and *when* you ask can be really important. Below are some tips that can make the process easier and more successful.

## Helping your child feel understood – Empathising

*How* you ask the question should give your child the message that you can see that they are worried and that you want to understand this better so that you can help. In contrast, asking 'Why [on earth!] are you worried?' may make a child much more reluctant to answer, as there is a clear message that they really should not be worried in this situation and that they are bad or silly for thinking the way they do. Using What…? rather than Why…? is a good starting point. Before asking a question, you could say, '*I can see you are feeling worried/frightened, that must be really difficult.*' This conveys the message that you understand that your child is anxious and that you know it is not nice feeling anxious. In order to tell you about their thoughts a child must firmly believe that you are asking because you want to understand the worries better in order to help them.

## Help your child feel normal – Normalising

Let your child know that they are not the only one who gets anxious: '*I remember when I got anxious about x*' or '*I know that your friend x gets anxious about y*' or simply '*lots of children*

get scared and anxious about different things. It's hard isn't it?'
Children with anxiety difficulties often say that they feel
different, that they think they are the only one with problems with anxiety. Using 'normalising' statements helps
them to realise that other people get anxious too.

Dad:    Ben, could you just pop upstairs and get your
        shoes?

Ben:    No.

Dad:    What is it that worries you about going upstairs?
        [being curious]

Ben:    I don't want to go on my own.

Dad:    That must be scary [empathising]. What do you
        think will happen when you are up there? [being
        curious]

Ben:    Nobody will be up there with me.

Dad:    And why does that worry you? [being curious]

Ben:    I don't know.

Dad:    I suppose if I had to go up on my own, I might be
        worried that if I fell over no one would be there to
        help me up. Is that what you are worried about?
        [normalising, making suggestions]

*Ben:*   *No, it's not that.*

*Dad:*   *And? [being curious]*

*Ben:*   *Well, I'm worried something will get me when I go up there and nobody will be there to help me.*

*Dad:*   *Is it anything particular that will get you? [being curious]*

*Ben:*   *Yes…you know…the monster*

## Make suggestions

Sometimes a child will just say they don't know. This can make it hard to keep asking questions and both you and your child can easily get frustrated. In this situation, we would suggest that you make tentative suggestions: *'Do you think you are worried that x might happen?'*, *'Some children worry that x is going to happen, do you think you are worried about that too?'* You can also encourage your child by talking about what types of things might make *you* worry in a similar situation. It can be helpful to make suggestions that you are confident are *not* what your child is worrying about. Sometimes the opportunity to correct you can make the fear easier for your child to talk about.

It is always important to present suggestions as a question rather than a statement, so your child can easily say no, that is not what they are worried about. Do not assume you know what your child's anxious thoughts are. If you already have an idea in your mind about what scares your child, then it can be easy to draw quick conclusions about what your child is telling you. Try to hold back on saying things like '*I know you are worried about x*' or '*I know you don't want to go to school because you are scared x will happen*', even if you are certain this is the case.

Always remain curious: What might my child be thinking? Could it be something else? Have I missed anything? Is there another way of thinking about this?

## Check you have understood

To make sure you have absolutely understood what is worrying your child, you need to repeat it back to your child and give him/her the chance to tell you if you have got it wrong.

Dad: *OK, thank you. I think I understand better now, but can I just check with you? [checking understanding]*

Ben: *Yeah, OK.*

Dad: *So the thing that is most frightening about going upstairs on your own is that no one will be there with you; and that is scary because in the film that you saw that monster was coming after children when their parents weren't around. Is that right? [checking understanding]*

*Ben:*   Yeah, pretty much.

*Dad:*   Oh, is it not quite right?

*Ben:*   Well, it's not just their parents. It's when any-
         one's not around. So, it's OK if Sam's with me.
         The monster wouldn't come then.

*Dad:*   Oh I see. So, the main thing is that if you are
         on your own upstairs then you think the
         monster may come and take you? *[checking
         understanding]*

*Ben:*   Yes, he'd take me to his cave and then I wouldn't
         see any of you again.

*Dad:*   I see. That does sound very frightening if you
         are thinking that if you go up on your own the
         monster will come and take you and then you'll
         never see us again. *[empathising]* I think I can
         really understand it now. Do you think I've got it
         right? *[checking understanding]*

*Ben:*   Yes, that's right.

## Am I putting ideas into my child's head?

'But hang on,' you may now be thinking, 'if I make suggestions to my child, won't that just give my child a whole

load of new things to worry about?' Our experience is that this does not typically happen – instead children sometimes feel reassured that, while they have some worries, they don't have that one!

## Pick your moment

The time *when* you ask about your child's anxious expectations may make a big difference to your chances of success. Sitting down with your child to talk about their thoughts works well for some children. However, for others, this can be difficult, and they may try to avoid talking or just refuse to talk to you. If this is the case, try to talk to them about their worries at other times when they feel that the focus is less on them – when you are in the car, walking the dog, doing the washing-up or cooking. Parents have often said to us that these times can work really well especially for older children. Also, don't feel you need to get all the answers straightaway. Ask a question here, a question there. Stop if you feel that your child is losing concentration or getting cross or frustrated. Try again another time or another day.

## Make it fun or rewarding

Talking about anxious expectations can be hard work, scary or even boring! It is important to try and make it a bit more appealing for your child or even fun if you can. For younger children, you can use dolls, cartoons, cuddly toys or other toys to talk about worries (see chapter 16). Help your child make a worry box or book to record their thoughts in – decorate it in their favourite colours. For older children, perhaps combine it with a trip to their favourite café and talk there. Maybe suggest your child can do something nice once you have talked a bit about their worries – watch a favourite film, have a favourite dinner, play a computer game together. It's important that your child gets used to talking about anxious thoughts, and that it doesn't become a chore for them, but rather a first step to feeling less anxious.

It can sometimes be tricky for children to describe their anxious expectations. Sometimes these thoughts pop into our heads so quickly that we hardly notice them, so do try to ask your child about their thoughts as they happen where possible, rather than much later on. On the other hand, your child may know what they are worried about but may find it hard to tell you as, perhaps, other people are present, and this makes them feel self-conscious. This may mean you cannot ask about the thoughts immediately, but try not to leave it too much later.

## Troubleshooting

### What if I can't find out what my child is thinking?

Below are some common problems in trying to identify your child's anxious thoughts, and solutions you can try:

*1. My child says they can't remember what they were worried about when I ask them later*

Try to ask them at the time, when they are actually worried or in the situation that makes them feel anxious, or soon afterwards. If this is not possible, try to get them to imagine in as much detail as possible being back in that situation again, or act it out together, and see if they can recall what they were anxious about.

*2. My child won't tell me what they are worried about at the time, I think it is because there are lots of people about and they feel uncomfortable talking about it*

Don't push them to tell you in the moment if there are reasons why this will be difficult; wait until a little later. See 'Pick your moment' for ideas of when to bring up the subject and ask them some questions about their anxieties.

*3. My child just says 'I don't know' when I ask what they are worried about*

Remember to try all the questions in the box on page 90. For some children, asking, 'What do you think will happen?' or 'What is the worst thing that could happen?' is easier to answer than 'What are you worried about?'

See section on 'Making suggestions' if you get stuck, but remember to 'be curious'. The table below may help – this shows some common anxious expectations that some children with different types of anxiety have. It may give you some ideas you can tentatively suggest to your child.

| Type of anxiety | Common anxious expectations |
|---|---|
| *Social anxiety* | I will get told off |
| | People will laugh at me |
| | No one will like me |
| | I won't have anyone to play with |
| | I will mess up my lines in the play/ performance and people will think badly of me |
| | People will think I am stupid |
| | I will get the answer wrong and everyone will laugh |
| | I won't know what to say and it will be awkward |
| | I will do something stupid and it will be really embarrassing |
| *Separation anxiety* | My mum will have a car crash |
| | Someone will break into the house while I am asleep |
| | I will get lost or taken by someone |
| | My parents will get really ill and die |
| | I will miss my dad when I am at school and won't be able to cope |
| | A monster will come into my room when it is dark |
| *Generalised anxiety* | I will do badly at my work |
| | I will fail the test/exam |
| | My friends and I will fall out |
| | I won't be able to get to sleep and will be really tired tomorrow – I will find it hard to cope |

| | |
|---|---|
| | Something bad might happen at school tomorrow |
| | There might be a flood and we all get hurt or die |
| | The plane might crash, and we could die |
| *Specific phobia* | The dog will jump up or bite me |
| | Someone will be sick at school and I will get sick |
| | The injection will really hurt, and I will get really upset |
| | The spider will crawl all over me and it will be horrible |

Another way of figuring out what your child's anxious expectations are is to observe their behaviour. Noticing what they avoid due to their anxiety or which situations make them feel particularly anxious can give you clues. Are there any patterns?

Here are some questions you could ask yourself:

*If your child is struggling to go to school, which days does she try to avoid the most? Does it involve certain lessons or certain types of activities?*

*Does your child avoid certain types of situations?* For example, those that involve talking to unfamiliar people, situations where they might be judged, or places where they might see a dog. See if you can notice any patterns to your child's anxious behaviour and use this as a basis to make gentle suggestions (see above).

*4. My child says they are not worried about anything in particular. They just get an anxious feeling, or they are worried they will get anxious because they 'don't like it'*

Some children simply worry that they will get anxious and will not be able to cope. Use some of the questions in the box on page 90 to get some more information and remember to 'be curious'. For example, *'What do you think will happen if you get the feeling or get anxious?'* It may be that the answer is simply that they will feel anxious and it will be horrible. If so, that's OK; it may mean that what they need to learn is that they are able to cope with feeling anxious.

It's not the end of the world if you can't identify your child's specific worry. You can still use the ideas in this book – but your focus will be more on building up their confidence so that they can cope if they feel a bit anxious, and on making steps towards changing their behaviour.

*5. My child keeps saying they don't want to talk about their worries, I think it might be because it makes them feel more anxious.*

Talking about worries is an important step towards finding out what your child needs to learn to overcome their anxieties. See the section 'Make it fun or rewarding' on page 96. Some children need a lot of encouragement to talk about worries and making it fun is a great way to do this. However, if despite your best efforts they still do not want to talk, then instead observe their behaviour and look for patterns to help you to develop some ideas about what they might need to learn.

## So, what does my child need to learn?

In essence, your child will need to learn that their anxious expectations are unlikely to happen and/or that if they do, there is something they can do, or they may cope better than they think/expect. Your main role is to support your child in developing a different perspective or point of view so that they no longer **expect** something bad to happen or expect that they will not be able to cope. This will help your child to be open to new ideas about what might happen.

It is important to keep in mind that sometimes children's anxious expectations are based on reality and you may discover, through putting them to the test, that the bad thing your child anticipated has actually happened and may happen again. For example, they might have given an incorrect answer in class, and everyone laughed, which made them feel understandably upset. In this case, the focus will be on what your child needs to learn (or do) to cope with and solve this problem situation if it happens again (see Chapter 11).

In order to find out what your child needs to learn about their anxious expectations, first of all write down the goal you are focusing on in the table opposite. In the second column, note down what your child expects to happen in challenging situations that relate to this goal. We have included some examples to help you.

You are now ready to decide what your child needs to learn in order to overcome their anxiety problems. This will be different for each situation you have identified. Have a go at filling in the third column, 'What does my child need to learn?' There is nothing magical or mystical about this – your child simply needs to learn that something else other than their anxious expectation might or could happen.

| Goal | What does my child expect will happen? | What does my child need to learn? |
|------|----------------------------------------|-----------------------------------|
|      |                                        |                                   |

Here are some questions that might help you:

- *Is the feared outcome as likely to happen as your child thinks it is?*

- *If the feared outcome does happen, will it be as bad as they think it will be?*

- *Might they cope better than they think they will?*

There are some examples to guide you on page 105.

Hopefully you now have an idea about what your child might need to learn to achieve the goal you are focusing on. If you haven't quite figured it out, don't worry; it probably means that you haven't yet figured out what your child is expecting to happen. You can still test out your initial ideas in the next steps. You might make some new discoveries along the way which will make what your child needs to learn clearer or may suggest that they need to learn something different from what you first thought – that is perfectly OK.

| Goal | What do I expect will happen? | What do I need to learn? |
|---|---|---|
| To regularly ask questions in class | I will get told off if I get something wrong; the teacher will shout and get cross | What will really happen if they get something wrong; what the teacher will do or say if they get something wrong; how well they cope if they do get something wrong |
| To go to school full-time | My mum will get hurt while I am at school and won't be there to pick me up | What is most likely to happen to Mum when they are at school; where Mum will be and what she will be doing; what Mum will do and what arrangements she will make if she can't pick up from school |
| To go to bed without calling us repeatedly to come up and say good night | I won't get to sleep and will be really tired tomorrow; I will play badly in my football match, my friends will be cross with me and I won't get selected again | What will actually happen and how much they will sleep; how they will play at the match, and how their friends will actually react if they don't play well |

**Key points**

- Ask open questions to find out about your child's anxious expectations

- Check you understand, normalise their anxieties, and remain curious at all times!

- Pick your moment and make talking about worries fun and rewarding

- Use your child's anxious expectations to decide what your child needs to learn

# Step 3: Encouraging independence and 'having a go'

Hopefully you now have some idea what your child needs to learn to overcome their difficulties with anxiety. Before we talk about creating opportunities for this learning, we are going to talk about some strategies that you can use to ensure that your child is willing to 'have a go' and to enter into anxiety-provoking situations to learn new things, rather than avoid their fears and worries.

## Promoting independence in everyday life

We have talked before about how anxious children often expect that they won't be able to cope in difficult situations and often avoid trying new, challenging or anxiety-provoking things. We have also talked about how we all learn through our experiences: we learn that setbacks and discomfort do pass, things are not always as we expect, and that if we keep trying, we are likely to overcome challenges. In order for your child to learn this, they need to have the opportunity to develop independence, to do things by and for themselves, in order to learn that they can cope, and succeed, even if it doesn't always work out well the first time.

Parents often have good reasons for worrying that their child might not be able to cope in difficult situations, and so it may sometimes feel difficult to step back and allow your child to try challenging things for themselves, especially if your experience has been that they get upset easily. As we have said before, we are designed by evolution to protect our children, and it can be very hard to resist the strong urge to help them out if we see them experiencing distress. Unfortunately, however, if we step in too early it may give the child the message that 'I don't think you can cope', or 'You need my help'. Instead, by supporting children to have a go at challenges, they can become more confident and independent in their everyday lives. Ask yourself whether you or others are putting a lot of effort into trying to protect your child or controlling the world around them to prevent him or her from failure or becoming distressed. Could your child be learning from you that you think bad things are likely to happen and that you believe that they can't manage on their own?

## Identifying activities for your child to try

The first step in encouraging your child's independence is to think about everyday tasks and activities that your child could try. It can be helpful to start with day-to-day activities, rather than anxiety-provoking activities; there will be less emotion attached to them, but they will give your child a general sense of being able to do new things and help them to feel 'grown up' and in control. Is your child as independent as their peers? Does your child rely on you to do things for them that they could actually do themselves (e.g. run a bath, pack their lunch, wake up in the morning)? What could your child start to do that they are not doing at the moment?

Below are some everyday activities that children engage in at different ages:

## Examples of age-appropriate tasks

| Child's developmental stage | Tasks they could be doing independently |
|---|---|
| 6–7 years | Brush teeth<br>Brush own hair<br>Set table<br>Tidy own bedroom<br>Collect post from communal area<br>Vacuum family room<br>Feed pets<br>Put on coat and shoes |
| 8–10 years | All the above plus:<br>Take rubbish out<br>Water plants<br>Care for own vegetable patch<br>Make a purchase in a shop<br>Prepare a simple meal (e.g. sandwich)<br>Wake up with alarm clock<br>Make bed<br>Prepare breakfast |
| 11–12 years | All the above plus:<br>Take care of personal belongings<br>Take short trips on public transport<br>Plan where family will go on a day out<br>Look up some information for the family on the internet |

Identify three activities (either in the list or other ones that you have thought of) that your child could try. Talk to your child about having a go at these over the following week.

## Tips for success

Here are some ways in which you can successfully encourage your child to engage in the independent activities you have identified:

### 1. *Show your child what to do*

If your child has not tried this particular activity before, demonstrate each step and check that your child has understood what to do. Then, let them have a go.

### 2. *Show confidence in your child*

Hold back and let your child have a go! Convey confidence in them with your body language. Even if they don't manage to do all or some of it or make a bit of a mess of it, praise them for having a go and let them know that you think they can do it (even if they need to practise a bit more or don't do it as well or in the way that you would like them to). See page 115 for more tips on how to praise your child.

### 3. *Reward efforts*

If your child is reluctant to have a go, it might be helpful to offer a small reward as encouragement. See page 119 for tips on how to use rewards with your child.

Independent activities my child can try:

| Independent activity | When did my child try this? | What tips for success did I use? | How did it go? What did my child do? |
|---|---|---|---|
| 1. | | | |
| 2. | | | |
| 3. | | | |

### 4. *Stay calm*

If your child gets upset, stay calm. Let your child know you understand it can be upsetting or frustrating when things are hard to do but encourage them to keep trying if the task is going to be manageable. If it has become clear that the task is too hard at this point in time, scale it back.

### 5. *Build up slowly*

If your child finds the task really hard, break it down into smaller steps. Get your child to complete the easier steps but perhaps help with the harder steps to start with. As your child gets more confident, help them less until they can do it all independently.

### 6. *Give choices*

If your child is very resistant to trying, don't give up. Remind them that you think they can do it! If they still refuse, give them a choice as to *how* or *when* (not *whether*) they do the task (e.g. do you want to make a Marmite or ham sandwich for your packed lunch? What time do you want to run your bath?).

### 7. *Share your own struggles*

Sometimes a child will feel overwhelmed by a task and get very frustrated or upset. It's helpful to share your own experiences of learning a new skill (e.g. When I was your age I found it really hard when I first tried to ride my bike; I found it helpful to practise over and over and get my dad to push me off until I could do it myself).

8. *Keep a record*

Complete the table of independent activities on page 111 to help you and your child notice and remember what helped.

## Changing your child's beliefs about being able to cope

Be sure to praise your child for having a go and/or for any successes they had. Ask your child how they thought they managed ('*How do you think you got on?*'; '*How well do you think you managed that?*'). That way, you are also getting your child to think about what they did and in doing so you will start to change their beliefs about coping ('*Yeah, I did a really good job*'; '*I did well, I don't need you to do this stuff any more, I can do it by myself*'). Comment on how well they coped ('*Wow, you did that without any help, that is so impressive!*'; '*I bet lots of people your age couldn't do that for themselves*').

It is also important to remind yourself how well your child did. Perhaps they can actually cope better than you thought?

## What if my child is already as independent as their peers?

Sometimes we come across anxious children who are actually quite independent and their parents struggle to find new activities for their child to engage in. However, with careful thought, we are almost always able to identify things that their child can do, that they are not currently doing in order to build up their beliefs about being able to cope and that they can do things themselves, without needing someone else to step in.

## Encouraging 'having a go'

Now that you have worked with your child on being more independent in everyday situations, we hope that they are starting to believe that they can cope with challenges and do things by themselves. Alongside this you can now start to work on helping your child to overcome their difficulties with anxiety. This will involve creating opportunities for them to learn new information that will help them to overcome their fears, building on the discoveries you made in Chapter 8. In order to learn new things about the situations they fear, they will almost inevitably need to be supported to enter situations that currently make them feel anxious and to 'face their fears' rather than avoid them.

In many ways avoidance may feel like a sensible strategy. For example, if Layla believes that by asking her teacher a question she will show her classmates how stupid she is, make a fool of herself or be ridiculed, then it's not at all surprising that she won't want to put up her hand in class. The difficulty is, however, that because Layla never puts her hand up in class she never finds out whether her anxious expectation is true or whether, in fact, her classmates wouldn't even bat an eyelid or, if for some reason other children are unkind, she can cope with it. So, Layla needs to ask her teacher a question in order to make these discoveries. Reducing avoidance and learning to 'have a go' is, therefore, crucial to learn new things in order to overcome anxiety. The following strategies will help you to encourage your child to do this.

## Attention and praise

Giving attention and praise is an effective way to influence children's behaviour. It is very easy to give attention to anxious behaviour. If your child is distressed, it's natural to want to comfort them and to try and calm them down. However, the danger is that your child inadvertently receives a lot of attention for their anxious behaviour. Paying too much attention to anxious behaviour can lead to a vicious cycle in which a child's anxious behaviour is receiving a lot of attention while non-anxious, 'have a go' brave behaviour is, inadvertently, being ignored. This is what happened between Ben and his parents, as shown in the diagram on page 117 (Figure 9.1).

Other examples include when a child who has experienced problems with friendships at school is asked 'Was anyone mean to you today?' rather than a more neutral question about how things were at school, or a question about anything positive that might also have happened with a peer; or at bedtime, where children often want to talk about their worries, and delay getting to bed and sleep as a result. Parents often ask us what to do at this time. They want to help their child with their worries but equally don't want to talk about them for hours! We would recommend that in these situations you acknowledge your child's feelings (*'I can see this is really difficult for you'*), but limit the time you spend talking about worries (*'Let's set aside 10 minutes to chat about this in the morning'*) (see use of worry time in Chapter 12) before you move on to something else (e.g. reading a book together).

Be mindful of the different ways you may be giving your child attention for their anxious behaviour, e.g. talking about worries or managing distressed behaviour or meltdowns, versus how often you notice or praise brave behaviour. You may need to shift that balance, and weigh attention more heavily on your child's attempts at facing fears, and praise these at every opportunity. For example, a parent of a child who has been struggling at school could get into the habit of asking the child to tell them one thing that went well at school, as well as anything they found more difficult, each day.

Praise needs to be clear and specific so that your child understands exactly what it is that he or she has done that you are so pleased about. Try to focus the praise on the effort they made that enabled them to achieve and the fact that they 'had a go' despite feeling anxious – not just the achievement itself. The extracts from conversations between Layla and her mum in the box on page 118 show examples of clear and specific praise.

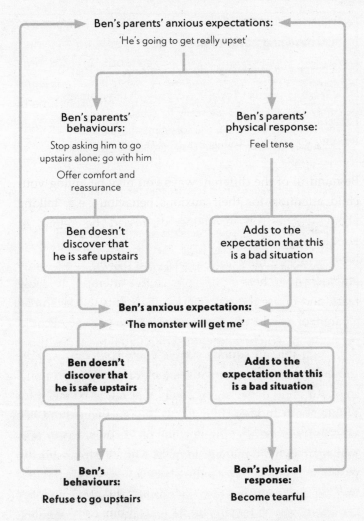

Figure 9.1 Cycle created when the focus is on avoidance rather than 'have a go' behaviour

**Encouraging Layla to have a go**

General and vague: 'Well done, Layla.'

Clear and specific: 'Layla, you did so well this morning when you got up and got ready for school without becoming upset. I know you sometimes have found Mondays difficult, so I was really proud of how you just got up and got on with it!'

General and vague: 'Your teacher told me you did well today. That's great!'

Clear and specific: 'Your teacher told me that you asked a question in class today, Layla. I bet that was quite a scary thing to do, but you didn't let that stop you. Well done!'

Although this all sounds simple enough, it can be quite difficult at times, as it involves looking out for and noticing your child behaving in a way that might be taken for granted with another child. For example, as you know, Ben was worried about going upstairs on his own. Every now and again Ben did manage to make a quick trip upstairs to grab something before running back down. This behaviour had been so swift but also so 'normal' (by other people's standards) that it had generally passed without comment. Once Ben's parents became more aware of this behaviour, they had two other concerns about praising it. First, they worried that they might make Ben more aware that sometimes he was facing his fear, which may make it more of a big deal and actually make him more reluctant to do it. Second, Ben's brothers were running up and down the stairs all the time and they weren't getting praise for it. It seemed unfair to be giving praise just to Ben.

Ben's parents, however, 'had a go' at noticing and praising Ben's efforts. They found that rather than the praise making Ben more aware that he was sometimes going up the stairs (and more nervous about it), Ben really appreciated it and it seemed to boost his confidence that he could go up the stairs without anything terrible happening. Ben's brothers appreciated that Ben had difficulties going upstairs, so didn't seem to think there was anything unfair about Ben being praised for doing this. In fact, they started to join in giving him praise themselves. Soon particular things started to stand out which each brother struggled to do (for one it was getting up in good time for school, and for the other it was getting homework done on time), so each boy started to receive praise for his own particular challenge.

## Rewards

In addition to praise, giving rewards is an effective way of motivating children to try new challenges, letting them know how much you appreciate what they have done and encouraging them to continue with that sort of behaviour. Rewards don't need to be expensive; in fact, they don't need to cost money at all. We are often struck by the rewards children come up with when asked to think of them. For example, Ben chose 'Going to the park with his parents' and Layla chose 'Making cakes' among their rewards.

## HAVING A RANGE OF REWARDS TO SUIT DIFFERENT ACHIEVEMENTS

You and your child will need to come up with a range of rewards to suit different goals. For example, if you were to reward a small goal with a huge reward then what will you do when your child achieves a huge goal? The worksheet on page 121 provides a space for you and your child to come up with a list of rewards together. Put down only those things upon which you both agree. For example, there is no point in offering your child a trip to the cinema if they hate the cinema; equally there is no point in setting up the trip of a lifetime as a reward if it is unlikely to happen!

## IMMEDIATE REWARDS

Try to come up with rewards that you are able to give to your child immediately or very soon after he or she has made the achievement, so that it is very clear what has earned them the reward. A reward also needs to be something that you will be happy *not* to give your child if the goal is not achieved. What would be the point of your child going to the trouble of facing the fear if they could have got that reward anyway? An example of a reward that is likely not to work out is *'If you can get to school on time every day this term we'll all go on a family holiday in the summer'*.

The first reason that this is unlikely to reinforce your child's 'have a go' behaviour is that the promised reward is too distant in the future. It will mean they may have, for example, faced the fear for a whole week with nothing good seeming to have happened at all. Children are rarely able to see such a distant event as an incentive. Second, it is likely that the holiday will need to be booked before the goal has been achieved and that it will be very hard to not go should the goal not be met. This reward is also a very big deal! If your child had an even bigger goal to aim for in the future, how would you top that? Finally, the whole family's holiday resting on his or her performance puts a lot of pressure on the child and, understandably, siblings would be very annoyed if the family holiday was cancelled. The consequences of this are likely to be negative for your child. Rewards, as we have discussed, should act as a bonus.

**Rewards worksheet**

*Tips to remember:*

- Make praise clear and specific
- Include a range of rewards under each category
- Rewards don't need to be expensive
- Make sure both you and your child agree to the reward

- Make sure you would be willing not to give the reward if the goal was not met

- Try to have rewards that can be given immediately or soon after the goal has been met

Things to do with my child:

Other things my child would enjoy:

## PROBLEMS WITH GIVING REWARDS

Parents sometimes have concerns about giving rewards to their children. The box on page 123 lists some of the common concerns that parents raise, along with our responses to them.

## Parents' concerns about giving rewards

1. *I don't want to bribe my child to do what I want him or her to do*

Sometimes parents feel as if they are manipulating their child by giving rewards and they feel this is wrong. We would agree that this may be wrong if the child is being 'rewarded' for doing something that benefits the parent and not the child. Here, however, we are using rewards to help the child to do something specifically because it will benefit them in the future. As far as Layla was concerned, asking the teacher a question could have only bad consequences (such as looking silly in front of her peers). Her parents, however, as adults, were in a position to see that in the long term she would benefit both academically and socially by being able to speak up in front of her peers. The reward they gave said: 'I appreciate that was hard for you, so well done for doing it.' The promise of the reward also tipped the balance for Layla as, in addition to the various negative consequences that she could imagine, there was now something clearly positive to be gained that would happen soon.

2. *If I start rewarding this behaviour, I'll have to keep rewarding it for ever*

It's true that when you have identified a behaviour as deserving a reward you do want to be on the lookout for that behaviour, so you can be consistent in rewarding it. As we have said above, however, rewards are used to help children do something that would otherwise be difficult to face. Once that task becomes easy (or even boring) it no longer requires a reward, and it is time to shift the rewards to other steps (see Chapter 10). The end of giving a reward for a particular behaviour can be framed as a positive thing, as Layla's mum said to her: *'You're so good at asking your teacher for help after the lesson now that I don't need to give you a reward for that but asking for help during the class will definitely deserve a reward!'*

### 3. *It's unfair on my other children who do this behaviour without needing rewards*

As we mentioned with regard to praise, children are able to understand that different children deserve rewards for different things, as they all have different things that they find a challenge. One family that we worked with had a great system in which the whole family earned rewards, and whenever any one of them achieved their particular goal pebbles would be placed in a jar. When the jar was full the whole family would have a shared reward, such as a family outing.

### 4. *Why should I reward 'normal behaviour'?*

Although the behaviour you are hoping to see may be 'normal' for many children, for your child it is a struggle and they need help and encouragement. In fact, the more 'normal' this behaviour seems, the more upsetting it probably is for your child that they cannot do it as they may feel 'different' or 'freaky'. As well as motivating your child to have a go, the reward will boost their self-esteem by showing that you recognise the achievement they have made.

## Observing others' behaviours

As we discussed in Part One, an important way that children learn to behave is by watching other people. Children often copy how other people act, so it's important to keep an eye on your own behaviour and take every opportunity to show your child how best to deal with fears and worries. This does not necessarily mean covering up fears and worries, which is hard to do, and in any case, children can be very perceptive and spot what's going on. Rather than trying to hide it, it may actually be helpful to let your child know you are anxious or worried about something (as long as it is an appropriate topic for a child to hear about, e.g. worries about a job interview or being late may be OK to share, but money worries or relationship problems may not be). In our experience, parents commonly let their child know they are worried about an upcoming interview or presentation at work or perhaps share their fear of dogs or another specific phobia.

If there is something anxiety-provoking that you are going to do soon, we would encourage you to talk to your child about it. Let them know what you are worried about but also be clear that you are going to do it even though you are feeling anxious. Modelling facing fears can be really powerful. Surely, if you are expecting your child to face their fear it is only reasonable that you try to do the same! When you have done it, let your child know how it went – in our experience, children will often ask before you tell them, as they are curious about what happened! Tell your child what you learned, did it go badly, or was it actually better than expected? If it did go badly, did you cope? Were you actually surprised by how it turned out? Do you need to try it again? Or could your child help you do some problem-solving (Chapter 11) in order to decide how to deal with this problem going forwards?

If the anxiety that you experience is so severe that you do not feel ready to face the fear, then think about who else might be able to set a good example in this particular situation for your child so that they get to see different (positive) responses to the situation that you fear. For example, if you are terrified of the dentist and are unable to contain this when in the dental surgery, think about who else might be able to take your child and set a good example. Make sure your child is clear that this is *your* worry rather than any reflection on their safety at the dentists. For more information on helping your child when you feel very anxious yourself, see Chapter 14.

## *Observing others' feelings*

Children also learn about how to behave from how other people react to what *they* do in different situations. For example, Sarah's parents were very aware of Sarah's fear of spiders. Although neither of them particularly liked spiders themselves, they were very keen not to show any fear in front of Sarah so that she wouldn't learn from them that spiders were scary. However (as discussed in Chapter 5), Sarah was on the lookout for any information that might support her view that spiders were to be feared. When a spider was nearby, Sarah's parents couldn't help worrying that she might get upset. Sarah picked up on the subtle changes in her parents' expressions and interpreted these as more evidence that, indeed, spiders were something to avoid.

At times anxious children can lead you to feel worried and frustrated. It is important to find ways to manage these feelings so that they do not interfere with the work that you are doing with your child. Chapter 14 focuses specifically on ways of managing your own anxiety to maximise the help you are giving your child.

## Have a go!

Now you are ready to start helping your child to take on new challenges to help them learn new information that will help them overcome their fears. Chapter 10 will talk you through how to do this in a way that is manageable for both you and your child.

**Key points**

- Identify activities for your child to do independently

- Encourage your child's beliefs that they can cope on their own

- Acknowledge your child's anxious feelings but minimise attention for anxious behaviour

- Be on the lookout for your child 'having a go'

- Praise and reward 'having a go'

- Set your child a good example of how to manage fears

# 10

# Step 4: A step-by-step approach to overcoming fears and worries

Now is the time to start helping your child to take on new challenges to help them gather new information that will help them overcome their anxieties. Ultimately, they will need to do the thing that makes them feel anxious in order to learn new things about what actually happens and to make discoveries about their ability to cope. Put simply, they need to face their fears! You will need to refer back to the goals you decided upon in Chapter 7 and to the discoveries you made in Chapter 8 about what your child needs to learn to overcome their fears in order to put into place the step-by-step approach that we describe in this chapter.

## Learning to face fears

Anxieties won't go away unless we face our fears and gather new information about our anxious expectations. If we always avoid or run away from things that we are frightened of, we never find out what happened, whether they were really as bad as we thought, or whether we could actually have coped with them. You will remember from the previous chapter that this is what happened to Layla, who didn't put her hand up in class because she thought that if she asked her teacher a question her classmates would think she was stupid.

The main idea behind this chapter is that by facing fears your child gathers new information. Your child, like Layla, may well discover that their fears are unfounded. Or it may be that your child learns that something bad does happen but that they can actually cope with it, or they may get the opportunity to develop new skills to handle it.

## A step-by-step approach

As our natural response is to avoid things that make us feel anxious, facing fears is a really hard thing to do. So, to Layla, the idea of putting up her hand and speaking up in front of her class was terrifying. If we had just told her to get on and do this she would probably have become distressed, not followed our advice, and may have been left feeling quite hopeless about becoming less anxious. One way to make it easier to face fears is slowly and gradually, step by step.

The idea of taking a gradual approach to doing something difficult is often familiar to children. For example, when we sometimes talk to children about how we should deal with a fear, they give us very good advice. The example below is taken from a conversation with a child in our clinic.

Therapist:  The problem is that I really don't like dogs. They make me feel really scared. But my good friend has a very big dog and it barks a lot and I would really like to go and stay over at my friend's house. What do you think I should do? I could just go round anyway, but it is such a big dog I'm worried I'll be so scared that I'll have to leave. Do you think there is anything else I could do?

Jack:  Why don't you go and play with a little dog first?

Therapist:  That's such a good idea. I do have another friend who has a small dog that doesn't really bark very much; maybe I should visit them first. Then when I've got used to the small dog I might not feel so scared about the big one.

## Making a plan

Drawing up a clear step-by-step plan with your child will help you both focus clearly on the goal you are aiming for. Remember, in Chapter 7, you decided on which goal to work on with your child and you put these in order of importance. You also decided on whether to focus on a short-, medium- or long-term goal to start with. Use this goal as the focus for your step-by-step plan.

Again, making this task fun by being creative about how you present the plan and using characters and colours to decorate it will help your child to feel a part of the plan-making. Create the structure for your plan first. For example, the plan could simply show a child moving up the steps of a ladder, or follow a rocket flying to the moon (stopping off at stars along the way; see figure 10.1) or a train going along a track (with the different steps marked as stations on the way to the final destination). Listen to what your child suggests and try to make the most of his or her interests. See the example provided below for some ideas.

## The 'Ultimate Goal'

You and your child need to work out steps towards the main goal that they are working towards, the 'Ultimate Goal'. In order to do this, you first need to be clear about what the ultimate goal is. As we have suggested above, use the goal that you decided to work on in Chapter 7 – What are your goals?

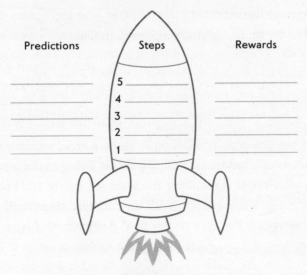

| Predictions | Steps | Rewards |
|---|---|---|
| _____ | 5 _____ | _____ |
| _____ | 4 _____ | _____ |
| _____ | 3 _____ | _____ |
| _____ | 2 _____ | _____ |
| _____ | 1 _____ | _____ |

Figure 10.1

---

### Ultimate goals

Layla:         To ask my teacher a question in front of my class.

Muhammed:      To sleep on my own in my own room all night, every night for a week.

Ben:           To play upstairs on my computer for half an hour when everyone else is downstairs.

Sarah:         To hold a live spider in my hand.

Alongside the ultimate goal, you and your child also need to decide on 'the ultimate reward'. In Chapter 9 you and your child came up with a list of possible rewards. Now is the time to go back to that list and find a reward that fits such a big achievement as reaching the ultimate goal. Write this down on your step plan alongside the ultimate goal.

---

**Ultimate Goals and Rewards**

Layla

Goal: To ask my teacher a question in front of my class.

Reward: Go out for dinner with Mum.

Muhammed

Goal: To sleep on my own in my own room all night, every night for a week.

Reward: Have three friends over for a sleepover.

Ben

Goal: To play upstairs on my computer for half an hour when everyone else is downstairs.

Reward: A day trip to a theme park.

Sarah

Goal: To hold a live spider in my hand.

Reward: Go to the cinema with a friend.

---

## *Breaking your goal down into steps*

Once you have your ultimate goal, your task is to break this down into smaller, more manageable steps that will gradually help your child make new discoveries and learn new information that will help them to overcome his/her anxiety and reach their ultimate goal. Think about what your child can do to help them gradually learn the things that you identified in Chapter 8 – 'What does your child need to learn'. We find it is useful not to have more than about ten steps (but you can have fewer steps), so that your child is not overwhelmed and can see the end in sight. It can also be helpful to start with a step that your child already does some of the time. It will be easier to get the ball rolling with the step-by-step plan if your child can quickly and easily have a go at the first step. What follows is an example of Layla's step-by-step plan.

As we can see, Layla's steps each give her the opportunity to learn a little bit more about what happens when she speaks up in front of others, to see whether her anxious expectations are accurate, and to build up towards the ultimate goal of asking her teacher a question in front of the whole class. The steps are ordered from the least to the most anxiety-provoking for the child. Don't fill in the predictions for the next step until your child has completed the previous step, as this is likely to change what they predict will happen for subsequent steps.

## Layla's step-by-step plan

**STEPS:**                    **REWARDS:**

**Ultimate goal**              **Ultimate reward**
Ask the teacher a             Dinner out.
question in front
of the whole class.

**6.** Answer a question       Go to the craft        **6.**
asked by the                  shop after school.
teacher (answer
not planned) in
front of the whole
class.

**5.** Answer a question       Stop off on the        **5.**
asked by the                  way home at the
teacher (planned              coffee shop.
in advance) in
front of the whole
class.

**4.** Ask the teacher a       Make cakes with        **4.**
question in a small           Mum.
group.

**3.** Answer a question       Choose a               **3.**
asked by the                  favourite dinner.
teacher (answer
not planned) in a
small group.

**2.** Answer a                Stop off on the        **2.**
question asked                way home for a
by the teacher                magazine.
(planned in
advance) in a
small group.

**1.** Ask the teacher         **Prediction:**        Praise from Mum   **1.**
a question after              She may think it is
class has finished            a stupid question
and classmates                or be cross with
have gone.                    me for asking her
                              something after
                              class

It's not always obvious which situations your child will find the most frightening, so it is important to ask them what they think. So that you can work out how to order the steps, ask your child to rate how scared he or she would be while doing each step, on a scale like this one:

| 0 | 1 | 2 | 3 | 4 | 5 | 6 | 7 | 8 | 9 | 10 |
|---|---|---|---|---|---|---|---|---|---|----|
| Not at all | | | A little bit | | Some | | A lot | | Very, very much | |

Figure 10.2 Worry scale

Use the table on page 138 to think of steps with your child, and ask your child to rate how anxious they would be about performing each step.

How anxious does my child feel doing each step?

Once your child has done this you can add them in order from the least to the most frightening to your own step-by-step plan, or you can use the rocket on page 133. On the following pages we can see Sarah and Ben's step-by-step plans, with rewards for each step, which may give you some ideas for your own plan.

| Steps to include in the step-by-step plan | How anxious does my child feel about this step? |
|---|---|
|  |  |
|  |  |
|  |  |
|  |  |
|  |  |
|  |  |
|  |  |

## Adding a reward for each step

We find it is helpful to specify all the rewards for all the steps right from the start so that your child can clearly see what they are working towards and what they will gain along the way. See Sarah and Ben's step-by-step plans (pages 141 and 143) for examples.

## Making predictions about each step

The main reason for getting your child to face their fears is so that they can gather new information to see if what they expect to happen actually does, or if something else happens. It is therefore crucial that you and your child think about what they have learnt once they have completed a step on the step-by-step plan. We find that the best way to do this is to treat each step a bit like an experiment. Ask your child, before they complete a step, 'What do you think will happen?' – a bit like a teacher might ask your child before they complete a science experiment at school. What is your child's prediction in this particular situation? Remember, their expectation or prediction may be slightly different for each of the steps on the plan, so it is important to check this out.

Also, your child may have more than one prediction about a step. This is absolutely fine. In fact, it suggests that they are already thinking about different possibilities rather than assuming only one thing will happen. Essentially, you want to know what they expect so you can review this with them after the 'experiment', to help them to notice any differences between their prediction and what actually happened so that they can learn something new. In this way, you are supporting your child in questioning their anxious expectation and helping them to consider alternative possibilities. You can see from Layla's step-by-step plan that her prediction for her first step (to ask the teacher a question after the class has finished) was: 'The teacher may think it is a stupid question or be cross with me for asking her something after class.'

Remember, only get your child to make a prediction about the next step they are facing not all the steps at once – this is because they will hopefully find out new information when they do this step, and this may well affect their prediction for the next step and so on.

## Sarah's step-by-step plan

**STEPS:**                                    **REWARDS:**

**Ultimate goal**                             **Ultimate reward**
Hold a live spider                            Go to the cinema
in my hand.                                   with a friend.

**5.** Watch a live                           Make cakes.        **5.**
spider without a
glass over it from
a metre away or
less for at least a
minute.

**4.** Watch a live                           Play a board game  **4.**
spider under a                                with Dad.
glass for at least a
minute.

**3.** Hold a dead                            A sweet from       **3.**
spider in my hand.                            the jar.

**2.** Look at a dead                         Praise from Mum    **2.**
spider under a                                and Dad.
magnifying glass.

**1.** Look at pictures        **Prediction:**  Praise from Mum  **1.**
of spiders in a                The spiders will  and Dad.
book.                          look yucky and
                               I'll get a horrible
                               feeling in my
                               tummy that
                               will make me feel
                               bad.

## Putting it into practice

So far, this chapter has been about how to put together a step-by-step plan. It is now time for your child to take the plunge and try the first step in the plan. As we mentioned earlier, it can work well to start with a step that you know your child can achieve – for example, something that they may have done before once or twice. Even though they have done it before it is essential to give the child a lot of praise and encouragement so that they feel encouraged to keep going with the step-by-step plan.

### Take your time

If the first step goes particularly well your child is likely to feel ready to rush on up through the steps to the ultimate goal. We would encourage you, however, to slow the pace down a little. It is important that your child feels truly confident at each step before moving on to the next step. Rushing ahead too quickly could lead your child to become very frightened by a step that they were not ready for, losing confidence and wanting to give up on the whole thing. Instead, we like to see that your child has learnt what they need to have learnt in order to feel confident enough to try the next step. If that is not the case, a similar step might need to be tried again. Your child may still feel a bit uncertain about the step, but this fear should no longer be overwhelming. It should instead feel manageable in order to continue up the step-by-step plan. Of course, you may not be able to give the same reward repeatedly, but be sure to continue to praise the achievement and, perhaps, offer a smaller token reward to acknowledge it.

## Ben's step-by-step plan

| | | |
|---|---|---|
| Prediction:_____ <br> _____ <br> _____ <br> _____ <br> _____ | **Ultimate goal:** To play upstairs on my computer for half an hour when Mum is downstairs. | **Ultimate reward:** A day trip to a theme park. |
| Prediction:_____ <br> _____ <br> _____ <br> _____ <br> _____ | **Step 7:** To read or play in my bedroom for ten minutes, with Mum anywhere downstairs. | **Reward:** Go ice-skating. |
| Prediction:_____ <br> _____ <br> _____ <br> _____ <br> _____ | **Step 6:** To read or play in my bedroom for five minutes, with Mum in the kitchen. | **Reward:** Go swimming. |
| Prediction:_____ <br> _____ <br> _____ <br> _____ <br> _____ | **Step 5:** To read (or play) in my bedroom for five minutes, with Mum at the bottom of the stairs. | **Reward:** Have Charlie round to tea. |

| Prediction:_____ <br> _____ <br> _____ <br> _____ <br> _____ | **Step 4:** To stay on the landing and read a book for five minutes, with Mum downstairs in the kitchen. | **Reward:** A new book. |
| Prediction:_____ <br> _____ <br> _____ <br> _____ <br> _____ | **Step 3:** To stay on the landing and read a book for five minutes, with Mum downstairs. | **Reward:** Choose a movie to watch. |
| Prediction:_____ <br> _____ <br> _____ <br> _____ <br> _____ | **Step 2:** To go to the top of the stairs and on to the landing, with Mum at the bottom of the stairs. | **Reward:** Two stickers. |
| Prediction: <br> I might hurt myself and Mum won't be with me. | **Step 1:** To go to the top of the stairs, with Mum at the bottom of the stairs. | **Reward:** A sticker. |

## Planning steps in advance

Some steps will need careful planning in advance. For example, Layla's step-by-step plan included her teacher asking her a question that they had planned in advance. Clearly some forward planning would be needed here, so Layla's mum made an appointment to see the teacher to tell her about the plan that she and Layla were following. Layla's mum took the opportunity to tell the teacher about the different methods that she had been using, and particularly what she found had helped Layla the most. Layla's teacher was happy to get involved with the plan and agreed to meet Layla before the start of class to decide together what question she would ask Layla and what answer Layla should give. Once she was aware of what Layla and her mother were trying to do the teacher was also able to be on the lookout for any signs of progress that Layla made in terms of speaking up in class and made sure to give Layla a wink or a smile. As well as teachers, try to get on board anyone who may be able to help and encourage your child, for example, family members, club leaders and friends. The more praise and support your child receives the better they will feel about their achievements.

## Reviewing each step

After your child has completed a step it is really important to check out exactly what did happen. Was it the same as your child predicted or different? What did they learn? By asking these questions, you are encouraging them to be curious, to spot new information, to notice differences between their predictions or expectations and what actually happened, and to start to think differently. They are then well on their way to learning what they need to learn to overcome their anxieties.

---

Useful questions to ask your child after they have completed a step:

1. What happened?

2. Was it the same as you thought? Did your predictions come true?

3. Did something else happen? What was it? Were you surprised?

4. How did you cope? (Were you surprised how well you coped with the step?)

5. What have you learned from doing the step?

---

This is the conversation Layla and her mum had after she had completed the first step:

> Mum: How did it go? Did you manage to ask the teacher a question?

> Layla: Yes, I did it!

> Mum: That's great, well done for being so brave and completing the step. What happened?

*Layla:* She answered it!

*Mum:* Can you remember what your prediction was?

*Layla:* Yes, that she would think my question was stupid and would be cross with me.

*Mum:* Did that happen?

*Layla:* I don't really know but she seemed OK and interested. She definitely wasn't cross. She was quite smiley.

*Mum:* Well, that's interesting, isn't it? Did you learn anything from doing that?

*Layla:* Not sure, I guess I can do it.

*Mum:* Yes, that's great. Anything else?

*Layla:* Maybe people won't be horrible every time I ask a question.

*Mum:* Yes, that's makes a lot of sense.

We would recommend that you keep a record of your child's progress with their step-by-step plan and also note down what your child has learned after each step (see table on page 149). You can also write down which strategies you used to encourage your child to 'have a go' (Chapter 9). Compare what your child has learned so far with the things that you noted that they needed to learn in Chapter

8. Notice how much your child has learned so far and what they still need to learn. If you were unsure about what they needed to learn, were you right or, in using a step-by-step approach, have you discovered they need to learn something different? You may decide you need to add in some more or different steps in order that they can gather some specific information about a worry or anxiety if your current steps do not allow them the opportunity to do this.

For example, Ben had completed all his steps on his step-by-step plan. Although he and his parents were really pleased, Ben was still very worried about going upstairs alone (even though he was now able to spend half an hour in his bedroom alone). When Ben's parents questioned him more about his worries and asked him what he thought would happen, he said he still worried that the monster might be in the bathroom. He said he made sure he played on his computer very quietly, so the monster did not know he was there, but said he could not go to the bathroom for fear of seeing the monster. Ben and his parents decided to devise a new step-by-step plan, this time trying to incorporate steps that would help Ben gather new information about whether the monster was in the bathroom or not. His ultimate goal was to go into the bathroom alone at night time, with a range of graded steps, including spending increasingly more time alone in the bathroom (from 10 seconds to 5 minutes).

Keeping track of my child's progress with their step-by-step plan

| Date/time | Which step did my child try? | What strategies did I use to encourage them to 'have a go'? | How did it go? What did my child do? | What did they learn? |
|-----------|------------------------------|-------------------------------------------------------------|--------------------------------------|----------------------|
|           |                              |                                                             |                                      |                      |
|           |                              |                                                             |                                      |                      |
|           |                              |                                                             |                                      |                      |
|           |                              |                                                             |                                      |                      |
|           |                              |                                                             |                                      |                      |
|           |                              |                                                             |                                      |                      |

## Safety behaviours

Safety behaviours are things that children might do to make themselves feel safe enough to have a go at facing a fear (as discussed in Chapter 5). These can be things like making sure they are not alone, that they have a particular object with them or that they are hidden in some way, such as when Ben played on his computer very quietly upstairs so that the monster did not hear him. Safety behaviours are common and can be helpful in supporting children with new or potentially anxiety-provoking situations, for example taking a favourite cuddly toy on a sleepover or school trip. However, if children become too reliant on them, they can prevent a child learning that they can cope in a situation because they believe they managed it only because of the safety behaviour. Be on the lookout for safety behaviours that your child might adopt. Although, for example, having a favourite toy in a pocket might help your child to face a fear the first time, make sure that they do not become reliant on this prop.

If your child does use one or more safety behaviours, you can use part of your step-by-step plan to encourage your child to gradually drop these. For example, they could do each step twice: first using the safety behaviour, then doing it without the safety behaviour.

Examples of safety behaviours:

• Speaking quietly or not at all

• Keeping head down in class

- Having a bottle of water to sip

- Taking a special toy to school

- Always saying 'goodbye I love you' to mum before she leaves

- Asking for reassurance that everything will be OK

- Checking school bag several times

## Troubleshooting

1. *My child became very distressed and anxious when I tried to get them to do the step*

Ask your child what is making them feel anxious. What do they think will happen? If they are very worried about something bad happening, you can get them to consider other possibilities before they complete the step to help reduce their anxiety a little. For example:

*Layla was scared that if she asked the teacher a question, the teacher would be cross with her and think she was stupid. Layla's mum asked if Layla thought that perhaps something else could happen instead. Layla wasn't sure. She asked what had happened when other children in the class had asked the teacher questions. Layla remembered that her friend had asked a question the previous day and the teacher had seemed pleased with her and did not get cross.*

Asking your child about what else could happen may enable them to face their fear and have a go at the step. Here are some questions you can use:

1. What has happened in the past or when you did x before?

2. What has happened to your friends in this situation?

3. What else could happen?

Alternatively, it may be that there is a particular aspect of the step that is too tricky for your child. Get them to re-rate their anxiety on the scale on page 137, to see if it is actually higher than they thought at first. If so, try to break the step down into smaller steps, with a revised plan to complete the easier ones first. For example:

*Sarah's first step was to look at pictures of spiders. Sarah got very upset. When her mum asked her why, she said that the cartoon pictures were not too bad, but she couldn't bring herself to look at the photo of the spider as she was concerned it would make her too anxious and she would have a nightmare about it. They decided to break the pictures down into steps, the first step would be the cartoon ones, then they would select photos which seemed manageable, before looking at the full set of spider photos.*

## 2. *My child refuses to do the step*

Ask your child if they can say why it is hard, what do they think might happen? As in point 1 you can ask them to think about what else might happen, using the questions listed. This may help them to have a go at the step.

Alternatively, ask them to re-rate their anxiety on the scale to see if it is perhaps higher than they first thought. If so, choose a different step or break it down into smaller steps that will help them to feel more confident in moving towards the original step.

If your child still rates their anxiety as relatively low, it may be that they are simply not motivated or interested in facing their fears. Review the strategies in Chapter 9 to encourage your child to be more independent and 'have a go'.

You should also consider whether your child is motivated to complete these goals? Can you help them be more motivated? Consider offering a different reward. Ultimately, if your child continues to refuse to try to complete this or other steps, you may need to review your goals. Did you decide to start with a medium- or long-term goal? If so, you may need to focus on a short-term goal first so it is more manageable and motivating for your child.

## 3. *My child has a tantrum when asked to complete the step*

Children sometimes have tantrums when they are feeling anxious, it can be another way of expressing anxiety. If you think this is the case, follow the tips in trouble-shooting point 1 above. Sometimes children have tantrums simply because they do not want to do something, and it is not related to their anxiety level. If you think this is the case, revisit the strategies in Chapter 9. Consider offering a different reward or a choice as to which step to try.

4. *What do I do 'in the moment' when my child is getting distressed while trying to complete a step?*

It can feel hard to know what to do when your child is distressed, and you may well feel torn. You could allow them to avoid completing the step, as you know this will immediately reduce their anxiety, but at the same time, you want to encourage them to continue, as you can see the benefit in facing their fears.

We would suggest trying the following:

- Acknowledge your child's distress – 'I can see that you are anxious or scared, that must be horrible/hard'

- Encourage them to continue to face their fear – 'You are really trying to face your fear and be really brave, keep going!'

- Let your child know you believe they can do it – 'You can do this, remember how you did x, I know you can do this'

- Get your child to think how they will feel if they do complete the step and remind them of the reward

– 'Think how pleased you will be if you do this, remember we are going to watch a movie if you manage it'

- If your child continues to be distressed, try not to respond to the distress (or give attention to this behaviour) and continue to show confidence that your child can manage – 'I am going to go into the kitchen now, let me know if you need me' / 'I am going off to work now, go and find your friends in the playground'

*5. What do I do if my child has a panic attack or experiences unpleasant physical symptoms of anxiety while trying to complete the step?*

- If your child is breathing very quickly or hyperventilating, encourage them to breathe normally if they can. Give your child the message that it is OK and that that these sensations are not dangerous, will pass and won't hurt them.

- Be aware that focusing on your child's breathing or other physical symptoms can sometimes make things worse. Help them to focus on something else. Listen for sounds going on around them, spot colours, and ask them to say these to themselves or out loud.

- For more information on managing unpleasant physical symptoms see Chapter 13.

## *When to call it a day*

Sometimes a child finds it very hard to face their fears and they may get extremely distressed. So, there may be times when you just need to call it a day. If you need to stop having a go at a step, then it is important that your child does not experience this as failure. Remember that we all have bad days! Try again on a different day, when perhaps your child is not so tired or is more motivated to have a go. Perhaps the step was too much too soon. Take some responsibility for this, for example 'I am sorry, it looks like we got that one wrong, and we need to do a different step first. Not to worry. We'll come back to this when we are ready.'

## Unplanned experiments

We have talked about encouraging your child to face their fears using a graded step-by-step plan. At times, you might also find that opportunities arise to face fears in a more spontaneous way. Here are some examples of opportunities that may arise (they could of course also be part of a step-by-step plan!).

1. Play in the park near some dogs while on holiday.

2. Ask the teacher what my homework was as I have forgotten.

3. Pay for something in the café.

4. Stay with my friend and her mum at swimming while my mum pops out to the shops.

As with a step plan, if you have the chance, check out with your child what they think will happen if they do this, what is their prediction? Offer a reward if you can (you may need to think of one on the spot!). Be sure to also check out afterwards what happened and what your child learned. Any opportunity to test out anxious expectations is likely to have an impact on your child's anxiety, so take these whenever you can!

---

### Key points

- Facing fears allows your child to gather new information about their anxious expectations

- Help your child to face fears gradually

- Draw up a step-by-step plan with your child

- Make predictions about each step and be sure to review these afterwards

- Agree rewards for each step

- Use one-off experiments

- Record what happens with each step/experiment and what your child learned

# 11

# Step 5: Learning about solving problems

Up to now the emphasis has been on helping your child to gather new information, so that they learn what they need to, in order to overcome their anxieties. To do this, you have encouraged them to face their fears in a graded way. Your child may have started to learn that their anxious expectation has not always happened or that they have been able to cope better than they thought.

Sometimes, however, your child may have good reason for thinking that something bad may happen – what they expect to happen may actually be quite likely. For example, a child who is being bullied would understandably feel nervous about attending school each day.

This is a genuinely difficult experience, a 'real-life problem'. It is completely understandable that a child will feel anxious in this situation and the problem needs to be solved. However, you might also be able to imagine this same thing happening to some children that you know and these children responding quite differently. One thing that is likely to make the difference as to how anxious a child gets is their own confidence in how able they are to make a difference to the problem. As we have said in earlier chapters, children who are more anxious are more likely to think that they won't be able to cope with a situation and will come up with solutions which get them out of that situation as quickly as possible (rather than coming up with a solution that will stop this problem from happening again). We want to help your child to be able to recognise when there is a 'real life problem' and to feel confident about getting that problem solved.

## When problem-solving is needed

So, as we have said, problem-solving is needed if your child faces a real-life threat or problem. For example, if your child struggles with maths, they may well worry that they will do badly in an upcoming maths test. In this situation, a problem-solving approach may be more helpful than simply asking your child to face their fears. If your child just does the maths test to see what happens, it may result in your child struggling and feeling anxious or upset about the result. They will of course need to face their fears at some point and sit the maths test, but may feel better equipped if they have come up with a possible solution to their difficulties first.

Bullying is another real-life problem that can be tackled using problem-solving. If this is relevant to your child, please also read Chapter 20 as we would recommend other specific action is also taken if your child is being bullied.

Another situation in which problem-solving can be useful is when you and your child have gathered information about a feared situation, by using a step-by-step plan, and your child has concluded that the feared situation is not very likely, but that it still *is* a possibility (for example, someone breaking into your house). This may continue to put them off facing their fears and keep their anxiety going, at least to some extent. Children sometimes say 'I know x is unlikely to happen but what if it did?' Problem-solving can be useful to help your child work out how to deal with a situation that, although very unlikely to happen, could still happen. Sometimes, having a plan for dealing with unlikely but feared situations can really help to reduce a child's anxiety further by helping them feel more in control.

Problem-solving may also be useful if your child reaches a step on the step-by-step plan that requires some organising in advance. For example, one of Sarah's steps was to look at a dead spider under a magnifying glass, but Sarah had neither a dead spider nor a magnifying glass! Rather than use this as an opportunity to avoid doing the step, Sarah and her dad used problem-solving to work out what they could do to overcome this difficulty.

## Becoming an independent problem-solver – asking questions not giving answers

When a child is very anxious it can be very tempting to try to solve problems for him or her. After all, as parents, we want to do all that we can to stop our children from becoming upset. But if your child is going to feel confident that problems can be solved, whether you are there or not, then they need to learn how to solve problems for themselves. This doesn't mean that your child can't ask others for help. Asking for help can be a good strategy for solving many problems (and is often essential, for example, in a bullying situation), but it is your child's responsibility to consider this solution among other possibilities and to be involved in the decision-making about the best way forward. For this reason, as we recommended when you were trying to figure out what your child needed to learn (Chapter 8), it is really important that you ask your child questions rather than give them the answers when you use problem-solving.

## Step-by-step problem-solving

There is a series of steps involved in becoming an independent and effective problem-solver. The steps that we describe may seem familiar to you, as many adults will use these steps automatically when they are faced with a problem. The steps are:

1.  Being clear about what the problem is.

2.  Thinking of as many solutions as possible.

3.  Considering the consequences of each possible solution and deciding which might be the best to try.

4.  Making a decision and having a go!

5.   Reviewing how it went and trying something else if necessary.

Following these steps will help your child to be clear about what he or she needs to do to develop this new skill. Eventually the steps will become second nature to you and your child, and it may not be necessary to sit and work through them all one by one, but to get to this stage we would encourage you to stick with the steps until solving problems in this way becomes a habit.

At the end of this chapter you will find some problem-solving tables to fill out, which will guide you and your child through the steps. We would urge you to use the tables and keep a written record of your child's attempts at problem-solving, because (i) having it written in front of you keeps it simple, as there is less to remember; (ii) it makes the process that you are working through thoroughly clear to your child; and (iii) should the same problem happen again in the future your child can look back at the table to see what can be done.

## What is the problem?

It seems obvious, but the first step is to find out what the problem is. The only way to be completely clear about this is for your child to describe the problem to you. You cannot assume that you know what it is. When your child has told you, repeat it back to them to check that you have understood. Whether you think this is a genuine cause for concern or not, it is clearly worrying your child, so it deserves your understanding, but you should keep the discussion quite matter of fact. We want to get across to your child, that, yes, you can see that they are worried and that there is a problem to be solved. So how is it going to be solved?

Below is an example of a conversation that Layla and her mother had the night before a supply teacher was coming in to the classroom.

> Mum:   *Layla, you have seemed much happier about going to school recently, but now you are saying you don't want to go. Is something bothering you?*

> Layla:   *We've got a supply teacher coming in tomorrow.*

> Mum:   *And what worries you about that? [ask questions]*

> Layla:   *He might be someone we haven't had before, so he won't know that I find maths really difficult and might get cross if I can't answer a question.*

> Mum:   *I see – so you are worried that he'll think that if you got a question wrong it must be because you weren't paying attention or something, rather than it being because you found the question difficult? [check understanding]*

> Layla:   *Yes.*

Mum: *This sounds like a situation you tested out before. I remember when you asked a question in class and in the end, you thought it might not turn out as badly as you feared. [reminder of what has been learned previously]*

Layla: *I know that the teacher might not ask me a question, and even if he did I might not get it wrong, and even if I did get it wrong he might not think I'm stupid. But I still can't help thinking, 'What if that does happen?'*

Mum: *Hmm, that does sound like a tricky situation. Let's have a think and see if we can come up with any things you could do to sort it out. [show understanding; set up problem-solving]*

## Brainstorming solutions

Your child may find it difficult to come up with solutions to problems; after all, maybe until now they have avoided dealing with problems. Or maybe their problems have all been sorted out for them. Whatever the reason, this step is all about helping your child to get into the habit of finding solutions. At this point you shouldn't care what the solutions are, or even if they would work; you just want solutions and lots of them! Just coming up with a solution – any solution – deserves praise, and every idea deserves to be taken seriously. The fact that your child is having a go at thinking of ways to overcome problems and anxiety is a positive and important step!

If your child really struggles to come up with any solutions, then you may need to give gentle prompts. But, as before, try to ask questions rather than giving answers or solutions. For example, 'What would someone else do in this situation?', 'When this happened before, can you remember what you did then?', 'If (a friend) had this problem, what might you suggest to them?' Or if more is needed, 'I know someone who had this problem and they did ... Do you think you could do anything like that?'

What follows is the conversation that Layla and her mum had to try to think of as many solutions as they could to sort out the problem of Layla having a supply teacher who would not know that she struggled in maths. If your child still struggles to come up with ideas, it's OK to make some suggestions. However, hold back on doing this until you and your child get really stuck. As we have said in previous chapters, if you do give suggestions, make sure they are tentative and are phrased as a question (e.g. 'Maybe you could do x, what do you think?'; 'How about doing y?') rather than a statement (e.g. 'Just do x').

> Layla:  I don't know what I can do about it – except stay home! [face lights up!]
>
> Mum:   OK. That's one solution. Well done. What other solutions can we come up with? [praise; asking questions]

Layla: *Send a snowstorm to my school so it can't open tomorrow.*

Mum: *Yes. Good. [laughing] Anything else you could do? [praise; asking questions]*

Layla: *I don't know.*

Mum: *What about your friend Jane? She struggles a bit with English, doesn't she? What does she do when there is a supply teacher? [tentative suggestions]*

Layla: *She had an assessment at school, so all the teachers will know that she needs help.*

Mum: *OK. So, making sure the teacher knows in advance might help. How could we do that? [asking questions]*

Layla: *You could write a note.*

Mum: *That's a good idea. Or is there anything you could do? Like at the beginning of the lesson? [praise; asking questions]*

Layla: *I could tell the teacher.*

Mum: *Great. Another really good idea. Well done. [praise]*

## *Which is the best solution?*

Your child needs to learn how to choose which is going to be the best solution to try. In order to do that he or she needs to consider (i) what would happen (in the long and short term); and (ii) how practical (or doable) the solution is. As you are taking all the solutions your child has come up with seriously, go through all the ideas one by one (even the seemingly silly ones) to find out what would happen and whether that solution would be doable. Once again, ask questions and hold back on giving answers. The box below gives some example questions to get your child thinking about the consequences of each solution.

Which is the best solution?

Example questions to ask:

'What would happen if you did...?'

'What would happen in the end?'

'What would happen to how you feel [about this situation]?'

Again, your child may not be used to thinking in this way. In this case you may need to prompt your child gently again. As before, try to stick to asking questions rather than giving answers, to help your child think about this for themselves. You will see an example of this in the conversation between Layla and her mum below.

Mum: *We've got lots of different ideas to choose from. So, let's think about what would happen if you did each of these things. The first thing was 'stay at home'. So, what would happen if you stayed home? [asking questions to consider outcomes]*

Layla: *I wouldn't be in the class, so the teacher couldn't ask me a question.*

Mum: *That's true. What else would happen? What would happen in the long term? [asking questions to consider outcomes]*

Layla: *Nothing.*

Mum: *Do you think that if you missed school every time there was a supply teacher anyone might notice? [asking questions to consider outcomes]*

Layla: *Yes – well you might. And my class teacher would.*

Mum: *And then what would happen? [asking questions to consider outcomes]*

Layla: *I'd get into trouble.*

Mum: *Hmm, maybe. And how would you feel next time*

*you had a supply teacher? Would you feel less worried? [asking questions to consider outcomes]*

Layla:   No. I'd probably feel the same.

Mum:   OK. Well done. Let's jot that down . . . Now, let's look at the next one: 'send a snowstorm'. What would happen if you chose that one? [praise; asking questions to consider outcomes]

Layla:   The whole school would get covered in snow and all the lessons would be cancelled.

Mum:   OK. And what would happen after that? [asking questions to consider outcomes]

Layla:   When all the snow had melted we'd all go back in, but I would have missed tomorrow's lesson.

Mum:   And what would you do next time you had a supply teacher? [asking questions to consider outcomes]

Layla:   I'd probably still be worried, so I'd have to send the snow again

Mum:   Wow. That all sounds quite amazing. Let's write it down... How about getting me to write a note to the supply teacher. What would

> *happen if you did that? [praise; asking ques-*
> *tions to consider outcomes]*

Layla's responses to her mother's questions about the other solutions are all shown in the example table, at the end of this chapter. Once your child has considered the possible outcomes he or she needs to think about which solution is actually going to be possible to carry out. Some example questions are given in the box below.

---

Finding the best solution

Example questions to ask:

'Is this solution possible?'

'So, would you be able to try this solution?'

'Is there anything that would make this solution difficult to do?'

---

With all this information, your child can then decide how good each solution is. By giving a number to each solution, it is then easy to compare the different solutions and choose the best ones. Your child should by now be familiar with using a rating scale. Use the rating scale on page 171 to rate how good each solution is. Use your creativity to help your child enjoy this, for example giving each idea a score by holding up a number or shouting it out.

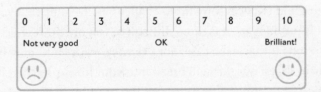

| 0 | 1 | 2 | 3 | 4 | 5 | 6 | 7 | 8 | 9 | 10 |
|---|---|---|---|---|---|---|---|---|---|---|

Not very good                                OK                        Brilliant!

Figure 11.1 Rating scale

As in all of the exercises, try to hold back your judgment and allow your child to decide how good each solution is for themselves. After all, if you decide that it is great, but your child has reservations, then they are not going to be very motivated to give this solution a try. The key is that your child is willing to try something out – if it doesn't work, that doesn't matter, you can consider an alternative idea next.

## Make a decision and have a go!

Once the possible solutions have been rated, taking into account the consequences and the practicalities, it should be relatively easy to see which will be the best one to try. If there are two ideas that your child thinks may be equally effective, try to help them pick one, or suggest your child tries them both out. Before they get started, check that your child has everything needed to put the plan into action. Have a practice run or try role-playing first. Does your child need to get anyone else involved?

Problem-solving can also be used for situations where

your child expects something challenging to happen, even if it is unlikely to. It is more difficult to test out your child's solutions if this is the case. For example, your child may be fearful that a burglar will break into your house. In this situation, it is impossible to try out the solution in the feared situation; however, you could act this out with them to test out if they think the solutions that they have come up with might work.

## How did it go?

After your child has had a go you need to check how they got on. Your child is likely to have gathered more information that will help to reduce their anxiety, so it is important to reflect on what they have learned.

---

**Review what happened**

What happened?

How did they cope?

Did they cope better than expected?

Were they able to make a difference to the situation?

What has your child learned from putting this solution into place?

---

If the plan of action did not work out as well as your child had hoped, help them to think about whether there is anything that could be done differently next time. Or is it worth trying another one of the solutions that they came up with? But do remember, no matter how it went, your child deserves praise for having a go at overcoming a problem.

## Troubleshooting

1. *My child can't come up with any possible solutions*

Make tentative suggestions. Ask your child what a friend might do, or what they might suggest to a friend, or ask your child what they have done in past situations that might have been similar.

2. *My child chooses an idea that I think won't work*

Run with the idea anyway (unless you are very concerned it will create a bigger problem or significant distress for your child). If the idea doesn't work, you can support your child in choosing a different one to try next time.

3. *My child had a go at the solution and it went really wrong*

Talk to your child about what happened and acknowledge that things do sometimes go wrong. If you can, tell them about a time that you did something that you thought was a good idea and it went wrong. But, don't dwell on it; move on, and consider other ideas that your child generated on the problem-solving sheet. Pick the next best idea and encourage your child to have a go.

## TABLE 11.1 PROBLEM SOLVING: LAYLA'S EXAMPLE

| What is the problem? | List all the possible solutions | What would happen if I chose this solution? | Is this plan doable? Yes/No | How good is this plan? Rate 0–10 | What happened? |
|---|---|---|---|---|---|
| Supply teacher at school tomorrow will not know I find maths hard and will get cross with me because he will think I was not paying attention | 1. Stay home. | 1. I wouldn't get asked any questions I would get in trouble with teacher/Mum I'd still be worried about supply teachers | Yes | 2 | |
| | 2. Send a snowstorm to school. | 2. Lessons would be cancelled. I'd still be worried about supply teachers | No | 5 | |
| | 3. Mum to write a note to the teacher | 3. I'd go to the class. If I didn't know an answer the teacher would understand and not get cross. Next time we could do the same thing and I probably wouldn't worry so much about it but I would need Mum to sort it out for me. This could be a problem if I don't know in advance that there'll be a supply teacher | Yes | 7 | |

| 4. Jenny to speak to the teacher before class | 4. I'd go to the class I'd feel a bit embarrassed talking to the teacher. If I didn't know an answer the teacher would understand and not get cross. Next time I could do the same thing and I probably wouldn't worry so much about it | Yes | 8 | I went in early and told the teacher that I find maths hard. He still did ask a question, but I could answer it! |
| --- | --- | --- | --- | --- |

**TABLE 11.2 PROBLEM SOLVING**

| What is the problem? | List all the possible solutions (no matter how weird or wonderful!) | What would happen if I chose this solution? (In the short term? In the long term? To my anxiety in the future?) | Is this plan doable? Yes/No | How good is this plan? Rate 0–10 | What happened? |
|---|---|---|---|---|---|
| | | | | | |

**Key points**

Help your child to define the problem clearly

Encourage your child to come up with as many solutions as possible

Ask your child questions to get them thinking about the consequences of each solution and how practical it is

Ask your child to rate each solution and choose which is the best

Ensure that your child puts the solution into practice

Encourage your child to reflect on what they have learned and praise them for their efforts

# 12

# Additional strategies 1: Overcoming worry

Worry will be something that is very familiar to you, not just because your child may be a worrier, but because worry is something that everybody feels at some time. Worries can go round and round our heads, causing more anxiety, and making us feel that there are no solutions, just more problems. At times, it can seem as if worry has taken over. Worries may have started to feel uncontrollable to your child and, even if they are briefly distracted, his or her mind may seem to wander back to their worries, the content of which may change from day to day. In the end, a large portion of your child's day may be spent worrying. The strategies that we describe in this chapter focus on the three main features of problematic worry: (i) that it spirals out of control; (ii) that it reaches no resolution; and (iii) that it is often related to uncertainty.

To take control of worry your child needs to be able to (i) put a limit on the time spent worrying; (ii) gather new information about worries and where applicable turn 'worry' into 'finding solutions'; and (iii) find ways to feel OK with uncertainty.

## Putting a limit on worry

### 'Worry time'

If your child seems to be spending a lot of the day worrying, or coming to you repeatedly with worries, then it is a good idea to set aside a 'worry time'. This is a fixed amount of time (limit it to about half an hour) when you and your child can discuss any worries that have come up during the day. The worry time needs to be at a time when you are both able to think; so not when your child is, for example, very tired or very hungry, nor when you are trying to get a million other things done. Choose a time when you and your child can sit and talk together without interruptions. Although parents often have some one-to-one time with their child at bedtime, this may not be a good time to talk about worries as it may disrupt your child's ability to settle to sleep, so try to schedule in worry time earlier in the evening if you can.

### 'Worry list'

Keep a record of worries somewhere safe so that you or your child can add to it with any worries that come up between worry times. So, if a worry comes up during the day, acknowledge the worry and make a note of it but otherwise carry on with what you were doing – this may feel harsh on your child, but as long as your child sees that 'worry time' happens they will soon be confident that the worry is not being forgotten or dismissed. Your child may take to this more easily if you can make the record special in some way – for example, use a special book, and perhaps you and your child could decorate it or stick on pictures of characters or celebrities that they like. Alternatively, you can make and decorate a posting box that your child can post worries into throughout the day.

Below, we will talk about planning how to test out worries and use problem-solving during worry time, but it is also worth noting that for many children just this act of saving worries until later can be very helpful. Children (and adults) can feel that by worrying they are doing something and if they don't worry things will get worse. Saving worries for later will show your child that nothing disastrous happens when they don't worry. Instead, through keeping a note of them, the worries can start to seem repetitive or even boring ('not that one again!') – and as a result, much easier to ignore.

## Cut out reassurance

Between worry times it may be tempting to offer your child some kind of reassurance that they don't need to worry. Of course, this is a natural response, but try to resist. Think back to all the times you have reassured your child and said, 'Don't worry.' Did that put an end to all the worrying? In most cases the answer will be 'No'. In fact, it is sometimes the case that when we are told not to think about something, we end up thinking about it more!

Try this yourself. Imagine a big brown bear sitting on your living room floor eating a jar of honey. Now – don't think about it! When you were told to not think about it did the image just come straight back into your head? For many people the answer would be yes. So, trying to *not* think about something can sometimes be unhelpful. In addition, as we discussed in Chapter 5 rather than giving your child reassurance, what you are aiming for is your child to be able to feel more in control of worries themselves, even when you are not close by.

## Distraction and focusing away from worries

So, you have made a note of your child's worry and now you need to 'carry on with what you were doing' – so how can you help your child to get on with something else? Basically, what needs to happen now is for your child to distract themselves and to take their mind off the worry until 'worry time'. We cannot stress enough that the aim here is not to ignore or avoid thinking about the worries but to help your child feel in control of the worries by being able to build experience of putting them to one side temporarily and then dealing with them constructively later, for example by gathering new information (Chapter 10) or problem-solving (Chapter 11).

You can distract your child in different ways. For example, try to create a game that will use your child's full concentration. If you are in the car, take a bet on how many red cars you will see before you reach your destination and get your child to count, or look at cars around you and try to make words using the letters from their number plates. If you are at home, find your child a job that will engross them and that they will enjoy.

Children often gravitate towards leisure and sporting activities which allow their minds to focus on what they are doing right then and away from worries. For example, lots of children enjoy bouncing on a trampoline or playing hide-and-seek or chase in the garden. Be on the lookout for activities that engage your child in this way and encourage him or her to do them at times when they might otherwise be worrying. For children to achieve in life, it is not all about academic or social success. They also need to have good, useful and effective ways of switching off and recharging their batteries. Worrying is not switching off, although trampolining may well be!

## Gathering new information about worries

We talked in Chapter 10 about facing fears to gather new information about anxious expectations. Facing fears using a gradual step-by-step plan often seems easier to put into practice where your child clearly avoids certain situations or events than when they are spending a lot of time worrying. When children worry over and over, they often worry about things that they might not be able to avoid easily, for example, how they will perform in a test or whether their friends will fall out. So, we need to think more carefully about how to gather new information about these types of worries.

# What are they worried is going to happen?

As we talked about in Chapter 8, you need to try to figure out what your child thinks will happen. Use the questions on page 90 to help you. For example, your child may be worried that they will fail a test at school, fall out with friends, that you will die, or that the plane you are travelling on when you go on holiday will crash. Children who worry often have a whole range of anxious expectations. It is important that you have a good understanding of what these are.

## *Carrying out experiments to gather new information*

One way to gather new information is to simply get your child to do an experiment to see if their anxious expectations are accurate. Make sure you get your child to make a prediction about what will happen before they do it, and then review what happened afterwards (see page 139). Sometimes facing fears to gather new information about worries is not straightforward – a common example is when a child is worried that a parent or carer might die. As we discussed in Chapter 8, the key thing to think about is what does your child need to learn? In the case of worrying about parents dying, we would not set out for the child to learn that the parent is not going to die – as they of course will one day and we can't possibly know when this will be. The difficulty of living with this uncertainty needs to be acknowledged (see below), but it might also be useful for the child to have the opportunity to learn about the probability of this happening and also what would take place if the worst were to happen.

## Other ways to gather new information

To get a clearer understanding of what your child needs to learn it can be helpful to ask your child to think about what the worst possible outcome for them might be if their worry did come true. So, for example, if they are worried about failing a test, ask them, 'Let's just imagine you do fail the test, what is so bad for you about failing a test?' They could answer 'The teacher will think I am stupid', 'I will have to move class', or perhaps, 'If I can't pass a test at primary school, I know I will fail my GCSEs'. Your job is to help your child gather information to see if their worst-case scenario is likely to happen or not. It may be impossible to be certain, but you might be able to gather enough information to decide if it is likely or not at all likely. So here, experiments might include talking to the teacher about how she views a pupil who fails a test and what she does; or doing a survey of adults who have passed their GCSEs and finding out if any of them failed a test at primary school; or even deliberately failing a test to see what happens. Once again, it is really important for your child to make predictions before they carry out these tests and then to review their predictions afterwards to see if they were true or not.

## Turning worry into finding solutions

Sometimes worries are realistic. For example, lots of children do fail tests from time to time, so what could your child do if they do fail this particular test? It might turn out that it is not a big deal. Or if they are repeatedly struggling in class it may be that there is a problem that needs to be addressed and that calls for problem-solving (see Chapter 11). Having a plan of what to do if their worry does happen often gives children a great sense of control and, as such, lessens the worry.

Finally, it is worth encouraging your child to think about whether their anxious expectation might also be an opportunity. For example, failing a test could flag up to the teacher that your child really struggles with this subject and so the teacher will arrange some extra help.

Ben's dad took the opportunity to help Ben devise a plan for one of his worries. In addition to his fear of monsters, Ben was also described by his parents as 'a real worrier'. He worried about many different things including war, terrorism and 'bad people'. Ben's parents had planned a trip to the city and he was looking forward to many aspects of it, but he could not help worrying that a bomb might go off while they were travelling by public transport. This was his 'worst fear'. This worry kept coming back to him. Even when he was doing something completely different it would just pop into his head and he would find it difficult to stop thinking about it. Ben's parents found it difficult to know how to respond to this worry, as it was true that terrible events like the ones Ben feared did happen sometimes, and Ben had seen reports about them on the news. No matter how much they wished it were true they could not honestly promise Ben that this would never happen. When Ben mentioned his worry, his dad made a note of it and asked Ben to post it into his worry box. They had the following conversation later on at worry time:

> Dad:   So Ben, we wrote down that you were worried about going out on Saturday. What is it that worries you about that? [finding out what Ben needs to learn]

> Ben:   I'm worried a bomb might go off when we are on the bus.

> Dad:   What makes you think that will happen? [asking questions to understand Ben's worries]

> Ben:   I saw it on the news. I know it might not happen, but what if it does?

> Dad:   That's a really frightening thought. So, you think that if we go on the bus we will get blown up?

        *(acknowledging Ben's fears; checking under-standing]*

Ben:    *Well, I know we might not, but I can't help worrying that we might.*

Dad:    *So, do you think we could find out somehow? [encouraging Ben to test his prediction]*

Ben:    *Well, we could go on a bus, but I don't really want to risk it.*

Dad:    *Can we gather any information to figure out how likely it is to happen before we go, would that help? [asking questions to help work out how to gather new information]*

Ben:    *I don't know. Maybe ask some people.*

Dad:    *Yes, we could, who could we ask?*

Ben:    *Maybe friends, family, ask if they have ever seen a bomb go off when they've been on a bus or a train.*

Dad:    *Great idea, like a survey maybe? [praising Ben for his ideas]*

Ben:    *But even if they say it's never happened to them, it still might happen to us.*

Dad:    *So it sounds like you think it's not very likely to happen but it's still worrying in case somehow it did happen. So, what if it did – what do you think we could do?* [summarising Ben's worries; encouraging Ben to problem-solve his worst fear]

Ben:    *If there was flying glass like on the TV, then we could duck down behind our seat, so it doesn't get us.*

Dad:    *That's a very good idea. Is there anything else?* [responding positively to Ben's ideas; encouraging more solutions]

Ben:    *We could call 999 on your mobile phone so an ambulance comes straight away.*

Dad:    *Yes. That's really good, too. So, we think it's most likely that a bomb won't go off, but it sounds like we have a plan just in case it does. Right?'* [responding positively to Ben's ideas; summarising and checking understanding]

## Feeling OK with uncertainty

Often, we cannot be completely sure that the situation we fear is not going to happen, particularly worries about our health and our family's health, death, war, disaster or the health of our planet. Your child can go a long way to reducing their worries by making predictions and testing out their fears and by coming up with a plan of action using problem-solving should the worst occur. However, there also comes a point where it is necessary to accept that sometimes we can't know for sure what is going to happen. At these times, your child will need to learn to live with the fact that there are some events over which we may have no control.

Children who worry often find it hard to tolerate not knowing for sure what is going to happen. They tend to have a lot of 'What if?' worries (e.g. What if I forget my lines in the play? What if the plane crashes? What if I don't pass my exams? What if I get ill or my mum gets ill?). There are strategies you can use to help your child feel more comfortable with not always knowing what's going to happen.

The key to beginning to get used to uncertainty is to face it head on rather than trying to avoid it. So rather than allowing your child to always know exactly what is going on (e.g. always having clear and predictable routines, and letting them know what is planned), it's helpful to begin to introduce some uncertainty into their life. This can be done through experiments.

Here are some examples of possible experiments to help children experience uncertainty:

• Organise for someone else to pick them up from school

• Plan a spontaneous play date

• Change plans for the weekend

• 'Forget' to add their drink to their packed lunch

## Managing worries about death and dying

Worrying about death and dying is common in children and often parents find it really hard to know what to say or do. Muhammed was worried that his parents would die, and he would be left alone. Muhammed's parents used some of the strategies we have described earlier in the chapter to help Muhammed deal with his worry. Muhammed's parents encouraged him to let them know when he worried about them dying and each time it was put on the day's worry list to talk about at worry time. It was a difficult subject for Muhammed's parents, as they could not help Muhammed come to any easy answers. Importantly, they managed to get a balance by being understanding of Muhammed's worries but also keeping a focus on what could be done to take control of this worry.

As it was a topic that could lead to more and more questions and be talked about for hours, it was essential for Muhammed's parents to keep to their limit of half an hour's worry time each day. After all, the worry could always be carried over to the next day's worry time if it came up for Muhammed again after worry time. As well as limiting worry time, they encouraged Muhammed to think about how likely it might be for one of them to die soon. They also encouraged Muhammed to think about his worst fear and to problem-solve what he could do if this did indeed happen. Finally, Muhammed's parents supported him in trying to feel OK with the uncertainty that it could happen and to find ways of coping with this. This annotated account shows his thought processes.

> *Both my parents are fit and well so the chances of them dying soon from being ill are quite low* [Muhammed gathered information about his anxious expectation], *but there is always the possibility that they could be in an accident or something* [Muhammed's worst fear]. *If that happened I'd go and live with my aunt. I'd always miss my parents a lot, but my aunt would look after me until I'm a grown-up and can look after myself* [Muhammed problem-solved solutions]. *Thinking about my parents dying doesn't stop it from happening and it makes me feel miserable and want to stay in all the time. So, seeing as they are alive, I should make the most of it and get out and do things and enjoy myself* [Muhammed finding ways to deal with uncertainty].

**Key points**

- Set a designated 'worry time' with your child

- Hold back reassurance

- Use distraction and encourage your child to engage in other activities

- Find out what your child is worried will happen

- Gather new information about anxious expectations

- Use problem-solving to make a plan to deal with potential difficulties

- Help your child to feel OK with uncertainty

# 13

# Additional strategies 2: Managing physical symptoms of anxiety

In Part One we talked about the physical symptoms of anxiety that children can experience, such as tummy aches, fast breathing and muscle tension. We do not generally tackle these unpleasant physical symptoms directly, as we often find that these unpleasant sensations go away as children change how they think and what they do. Sometimes, however, the physical symptoms that a child experiences cause a great deal of distress and it can be helpful for a child to learn that (i) these physical symptoms are not harmful; (ii) they will reduce on their own; and (iii) your child can take control of them if they need to.

## Recognising physical symptoms of anxiety

Often children are not aware that the physical symptoms that they are experiencing are in fact due to anxiety.

Children will often complain of tummy aches, headaches, feeling hot etc. and think that they are physically unwell.

---

**Common physical symptoms of anxiety in children**

Headaches

Tummy aches

Nausea (or even being sick)

Shaking

Dizziness

Sweating

Fast heart beat

Breathing quickly

Tingling

Dry/tight throat

Tight muscles

---

Parents also often struggle to know if their child's symptoms are due to anxiety or to a physical health problem. Sometimes parents might worry that their child is 'making up' these symptoms in order to avoid something they are anxious about. In our experience, children are generally actually experiencing these symptoms, but this may be a consequence of anxiety. It is therefore important to acknowledge these unpleasant feelings but also to help your child see them as a symptom of anxiety (not a sign of a physical catastrophe). Help your child to notice patterns in when these symptoms come along – are they often before school or particular activities? It might also be helpful to share some examples of times that you have experienced physical symptoms of anxiety, for example having butter-flies in your stomach before an exam, or your driving test.

## How to respond to your child's physical sensations of anxiety

Many children are able to ignore physical symptoms once they are satisfied that these are signs of anxiety and not a serious physical health problem. However, other children may still find that these symptoms become the centre of their attention. Unfortunately, a vicious cycle can easily arise in which your child gets the symptoms when they become anxious but then become more anxious when they notice the symptom. (see page 43 in Part 1 – 'Vicious cycle of physical symptoms').

To avoid getting into this cycle, try not to give too much attention to these symptoms. If your child mentions them, check you understand and acknowledge that it is probably quite unpleasant – *'so you feel your heart beating fast, that can't be very nice'* – and then move on. Talk about some-thing else or try to distract your child by playing a game, doing an activity together, or getting them to help you with some chores. For most children, that will be enough to focus their attention on to something else and to stop the vicious cycle from starting.

## Shifting the focus of attention away from physical symptoms

Some children may have already got themselves in to a pattern of focusing on and/or worrying about their physical symptoms and so it may be hard to simply distract them. In this case it may be helpful to spend some time helping them to learn to shift their attention away from their physical symptoms to investigate how this affects how anxious they feel. Sit down with your child and get them to focus on something in their surroundings for about 30 seconds to start with. For example, you can ask them to notice all the different colours around them, or sounds, or even textures – whatever you both agree on. Here is an example of how Sarah's dad helped her move her focus away from her physical symptoms.

> Dad:    *OK, I want to you try and focus on some things around you and not on how your body is feeling right now. I know it might be hard, but it will help you feel a bit calmer. Let's just look around and try and spot as many different colours as we can. Why don't you say them all out loud?*
>
> Sarah:   *Blue, green, red, orange, the cat is black…*

*Dad:* Great, what other colours can you see?' I bet you can't spot 10!

*Sarah:* That's a funny brown colour, grey, oh, white... purple, your top is, um, turquoise.

*Dad:* Well spotted. I noticed some light blue books on the bookshelf too, and a red package on the table. How about we listen for sounds now? See how many you can hear?

*Sarah:* OK, but I am still feeling anxious... my heart is still beating fast.

*Dad:* Let's try really hard to listen for sounds then and not pay too much attention to your anxiety.... right, what can you hear?

*Sarah:* Birds, um, the washing machine I think, um, rain, something peeping, maybe the fridge... I heard someone talking I think?

*Dad:* You're doing a great job, how are you feeling?

*Sarah:* A bit better, my heart is not so fast.

*Dad:* OK, shall we go and take the dog for a walk, maybe we can spot more things out and about?

Keep it short so that they can keep paying attention. Do it as well yourself so you know what your child is experiencing, and you can compare notes! Tell your child that you want them to focus completely on colours, for example. This might sound easier said than done but practice will help them (and you!) get better at it. Your child might want to say the colours to themselves as they spot them, at least to start with. After 30 seconds, ask your child how they got on. Did they manage to just focus on the colours or might they need a bit more practice?

The above exercise might be enough to help your child feel calmer. However, with older children, encourage your child to do an experiment to test what difference it makes when they focus on their anxious symptoms compared to when they focus on what is going on around them. Encourage your child to try to switch between focusing on something in their surroundings (remember to be specific – sounds, colours, smells etc.) for say 30 seconds, and then focusing completely on their body and what is happening, for a further 30 seconds. Encourage them to switch back again to their surroundings for a final 30 seconds. What do they notice? Did they feel more anxious focusing on their surroundings or on their body?

Most children will say they feel less anxious when they focus outside of their body on the environment around them. Once your child is able to focus really well on their surroundings when they are not feeling particularly anxious, they can begin to try to use this strategy when they are feeling anxious. No doubt it will be harder to do when they are anxious to start with, but with practice, most children get really good at switching their attention away from their physical sensations and their body to other things around them. In turn, their anxiety tends to reduce and their physical symptoms are also likely to reduce.

## Relaxation training

Traditionally, relaxation techniques have been used to manage the physical symptoms of anxiety, which include deep breathing, but also some other techniques, such as muscle relaxation and visualisation. Some children and families enjoy using these types of strategies; however, we have not included them in this book for the following reasons:

1. There is not clear evidence that the physical reactions of children with anxiety difficulties are different to those of other children.

2. It is important for children to fully experience their anxiety (including any physical symptoms) in order to truly face their fears and overcome them.

3. Relaxation techniques do not seem to improve outcomes for children with anxiety difficulties.

4. We have found that parents and children rarely practise relaxation techniques at home and often find it hard to do so.

Key points

- Help your child to spot physical symptoms of anxiety and to learn that they are harmless

- Distract your child to help them to move the focus of their attention away from their symptoms

- Show your child that they have control over their symptoms, for example, by learning to switch their attention away from their physical sensations

# 14

# Additional strategies 3: Managing your own anxiety

As we discussed in Chapter 4, there are likely to be several factors that have led to your child becoming anxious. It doesn't necessarily matter what originally *caused* your child to be anxious. What does matter, however, are any factors that may be keeping their anxiety going or getting in the way of you helping your child overcome his or her anxiety.

As we said at the beginning of Part Two, parents of children who have difficulties with anxiety are more likely to have difficulties with anxiety themselves than parents of non-anxious children. Applying the principles in this book might be particularly challenging or daunting if you have a tendency to feel anxious yourself. However, children whose parents are anxious can do very well using the strategies in this book, and actually when children improve many parents experience a reduction in their own anxiety, too. This may be because life has become so much easier as a result of their child's improvements or because parents are encouraged to tackle their own anxieties as they help their children.

It may be helpful for your child if you can try to tackle your own anxiety while also supporting your child. There are three main reasons why this might be helpful: your child may start to learn new ways of thinking and behaving from you, you may find it easier to follow this programme, and you will be a great role model for your child – your child may be more likely to be willing to work on their anxiety and to enter into anxiety-provoking situations if they know you are doing the same thing. Therefore, if you experience a lot of anxiety yourself, by making a concerted effort to overcome this you will not only be helping yourself, but you may also be helping your child.

We have sometimes seen some advantages of having a parent who has experience of anxiety difficulties support-ing their child's treatment. For example, you may be more likely to understand your child's position, and to really get how they are feeling; you are likely to recognise how hard it is to tackle anxieties and in doing so you are likely to be empathetic and sensitive in your approach; and you are in a great position to normalise your child's fears by sharing appropriate anxieties of your own.

However, parents have also told us that their own anx-ieties can present challenges when it comes to supporting their child. For example, your child may be aware that you worry a lot about them and so they may be reluctant to share their own worries with you; you may inadvertently give your child anxious signals or messages about the world around them; your child may see you responding to challenges with avoidance; and you may have certain expectations about how your child will react in challenging situations that are influenced by your own fears or worries. In addition, if difficulties with anxiety make it hard for you to take part in certain activities or be in certain situations, your child may have fewer opportunities to face their fears. In this chapter, we talk about how to spot these potential challenges and how to overcome them.

Our focus in this chapter is about how to prevent anxiety that you experience causing difficulties for you in supporting your child. While many of the strategies we describe in this book may be helpful for you, you may find it useful to read other titles in this series and the Overcoming Series for more extensive advice on overcoming your own difficulties with anxiety (see Useful Resources, page 305).

## Worries about your child

Having a child is worrying. Having an anxious child is more worrying. Having an anxious child when you are already an anxious person yourself – well, it's clearly not going to be easy! It is normal to worry about your child, but as with all worries, if they are getting in the way of you parenting your child in the way that you would like to, then these worries need tackling. If your child is aware of the extent that you worry about them he or she may not want to be open with you about their worries for fear of upsetting you further. You need to be able to show your child that you can deal with their worries. See Chapter 8 for more ideas on how to encourage your child to talk about their worries. Be mindful of your reaction, both what you say and how you appear. The next section talks more about how to deal with this.

It is important to note, however, that this does not mean you should cover up all your worries and pretend they don't exist. Children often say that they feel like they are the only one that feels the way they do, they feel they are 'different' or 'weird' for feeling scared all the time. Often, they are not aware that *everyone* has fears and that *everyone* feels scared sometimes. Rather than hiding all your fears from your child it is important to show that having fears is normal and that there are ways of dealing with them so that they don't take over your life.

## Messages you give about the world through your own fears

Children inevitably learn how to think about the world from the people around them. If a parent thinks about the world in an anxious way, this may encourage a child to do the same, particularly if they are a more sensitive, cautious or anxious child. On the other hand, if a parent can set an example for a child of how to approach anxious expectations in a different way this can help the child learn new ways of seeing the world. So, rather than trying to cover up your fears, use them as an opportunity to set a good example, if you can. Think about a fear that is appropriate to share with your child (for example, a fear of cats rather than something of an adult nature such as money or relationships worries) and show your child how you can use the strategies in this book to tackle it.

Sometimes parents do not feel able or ready to tackle a particular fear; if this is the case and you feel you really can't face a particular fear at this time, then try to get someone else involved who can help your child experience the things you fear, so that they can see that it is 'your fear' rather than being something that is actually dangerous, and they get the opportunity to see that they can cope with it. For example, this might mean asking someone else to take them to the dentist, to the swimming pool, or to stroke a dog. The way that you talk about fears will also help with this. For example, Layla was perfectly aware that her mother had a fear of cats. However, Layla's mum had never stopped Layla stroking cats or playing with cats that belonged to other people. Layla's mum would say to her, 'It's just me that doesn't like cats, a lot of people love them.' Because Layla had been able to have her own positive experiences with cats, despite her mother's fear, Layla did not share the fear. From her mum letting her know that different people felt differently about cats and from having the opportunity to play with cats, she did not think of her mum's fear as a sign that 'cats are scary and dangerous'; instead she thought of it as 'just Mum's funny worry'. How you discuss your fears or worries with your child is, therefore, very important. In particular, they need to be talked about as 'just' fears or worries rather than as facts.

## Anxious signals and messages

Worries, both about things going on in your own life and about your child, can sometimes 'leak out', and be visible to others. You need to be on the lookout for subtle expressions of anxiety when you are with your child. For example, despite maintaining a calm manner, do you cross the road whenever a dog approaches? Or, despite being hospitable to your new neighbours when they visit, would you still express relief when they have gone home? These are examples of ways we may unwittingly display signs of our own anxiety. Ask a friend, partner or relative to watch you when you encounter a stressful situation with your child. Can they help you spot whether your anxious feelings are showing themselves and getting in the way of you helping your child?

## Do as I do

Your child may not just be noticing how you react when *he or she* faces a fear. They may also be picking up on how *you* react to things that make you feel anxious. If a child sees a parent dealing with fears by trying to avoid them, rather than facing up to them, then it is likely that the child will learn to do the same (particularly if the child is prone to anxiety). On the other hand, if a parent can show a child that they are able to face fears and overcome them then this will serve as encouragement to the child to do the same. This, of course, is not always easy; but it is fine for your child to see that you too are experiencing difficulty, as they will also undoubtedly struggle at times to overcome fears.

## What do you expect of your child?

As we have said, anxious children will present a worry to their parents, but if a parent already tends to experience a lot of anxiety this is likely to be amplified. We have found that parents who think in an anxious way tend to expect their child to see the world in a similar way and, as we have described above, how parents think about their child will, of course, influence how they behave with their child.

In Chapter 9 we talked about Sarah's parents, who were really worried that Sarah might become upset and not be able to cope if she saw a spider. These negative expectations about how Sarah would react understandably influenced her parents' behaviour. Sarah picked up on the little changes in her parents' expressions when they spotted a spider and interpreted these as more evidence that spiders were, indeed, something to be feared. This vicious cycle is shown in Figure 14.1, overleaf.

**Trigger: Sarah's parents spot a spider in the room**

Figure 14.1 How expectations affect how children think and feel

Our expectations as parents can also influence how we respond to our children in other ways. As we have said before, parents are designed by evolution to protect their children, so if, for example, you think your child is going to get very upset, of course you are likely to want to do what you can to stop this from happening. You may want to remove them from the situation and provide reassurance that they will be all right. On the other hand, you may expect that they are going to make a big fuss and then feel annoyed or irritated and become snappy or cross with your child. Although both of these reactions are completely understandable, they are likely to get in the way of the work you are doing to help your child overcome their fears, worries and anxiety.

> *Layla's mum, like Layla, often became very anxious about what other people thought of her. She found it extremely difficult, therefore, when Layla started to make a fuss about going into school at the school gates. It seemed to her that all the other children were going in fine, it was just her child making a fuss, and all the other parents must be watching and thinking she was a useless parent. Now, as they approached the school gates Layla's mum started to feel her fear that Layla was going to make a scene creep up on her. She found it difficult to concentrate on her plan of how she was going to manage Layla's fear, as she was getting overwhelmed by her own anxiety. When Layla spoke to her she couldn't help snapping back at her. She could see that this was not helping Layla feel positively about going into school.*

Both Layla's mum and Sarah's parents identified their own anxious thoughts about their children's reactions, and thought about what *they* needed to learn about their children and their fears. What they came up with is shown on the following pages.

| Goal | What am I expecting to happen? | What do I need to learn or discover? |
|------|-------------------------------|--------------------------------------|
| To be able to remain calm and positive when Sarah sees a spider. | I am worried Sarah will get really upset when she sees a spider and won't be able to cope. | What actually happens if Sarah sees a spider? Will she be able to cope? Are there things we can do to help her cope? Will we be able to see/notice if she copes well? |

| Goal | What am I expecting to happen? | What do I need to learn or discover? |
|------|-------------------------------|--------------------------------------|
| To be able to remain calm and not snap when we reach the school gates. To be able to concentrate on our plan of action. | Layla will get really upset, shout and cry, and the other parents will think that I am a terrible parent. | What will actually happen when we get to the school gate if I stick to my plan? Will Layla be able to manage? If she doesn't will other parents judge me? (Maybe they will sympathise?) |

## Creating the right opportunities

We need to create the opportunities for our children to be able to face their fears. This may mean liaising with a teacher (as we saw in Layla's step-by-step plan, Chapter 11) or other people who may be able to help, or collecting materials (like dead and alive spiders, as we did in Sarah's step-by-step plan). For some parents, feelings of anxiety may make these sorts of things hard to do. For example, Layla's mum felt anxious in social situations, in particular those where she felt others were judging her. Approaching Layla's teacher was, therefore, quite a difficult thing for her to do. Similarly, Sarah's parents weren't that keen on spiders, so the job of collecting spiders was not something that they relished. Here is another area, then, where it is important to be aware of whether your own anxiety could get in the way of what you are trying to do to help your child move forward. If it is, then maybe the task you need to do to help your child could form your own goal. Or, if facing these fears is really out of the question right now, enlist someone else who can help create the right opportunities for your child to face their fears.

## Overcoming your own fears and worries

As we discussed earlier in the book, experiencing anxiety is a normal thing – it happens to everyone. The point at which it becomes a problem, however, is when it starts getting in the way of your life – your work, your friendships, your family and your parenting. We have talked above

| | Short-term | Medium-term | Long-term |
|---|---|---|---|
| Goal 1 | | | |
| Goal 2 | | | |
| Goal 3 | | | |

about ways in which your anxiety might make it difficult for you to help your child overcome their fears. If you recognise that anxiety is getting in the way of you helping your child and stopping you from doing what you would like to be doing, it is worth considering whether now is the time to address your own fears and worries.

You can start by using this table to write down your goals for overcoming your own fears and worries (refer back to Step 1 to guide you). These may be influenced by some of the suggestions we have made earlier in this chapter.

The strategies that have been discussed in this book are not used exclusively with children or young people, but are similar to strategies that adults can use. You will find more information in other books listed in the Useful Resources section at the end of the book; however, the box below summarises the main strategies we have focused on.

*1. What are your goals?*

What do you want to work on, in the short, medium and long term?

*2. What do you need to learn?*

How are you thinking about situations and people that you come across? Are you expecting the worst? Are you seeing possible danger all around you? What do you need to learn to overcome your anxieties and achieve your goals?

On page 105 you will find a similar chart to the one you used with your child in Chapter 8. This time try using the chart to consider one of your goals.

*3. A step-by-step approach to overcoming fears and worries*

What do you need to do to test your fears and learn new things about yourself and/or the world? Would it help to face the fear gradually? If so, make your own step-by-step plan. Reward yourself for your progress and encourage others to reward you, too.

*4. Overcoming problems*

Do you feel paralysed when confronted with a problem? Instead, try to focus on solutions. What are all the possible things you could do (no matter how silly)? What would happen if you did these things? What will be the best solution? Give it a try and see how it goes.

*5. Overcoming worry*

Do your worries spiral out of control? Put a limit on worrying. Allocate a set time to your worries and use this time to find solutions. Shift your focus of attention away from worrying outside of these times. During worry time, work out what your worst fear is, gather new information about your expectations, use problem-solving to plan for challenges and find ways to feel OK with uncertainty.

## Getting your child involved

Showing your child that you are facing your fears can give them a really powerful message – so don't hide the fact you are facing them. Talk to your child about what you are doing. They may be able to help you, for example, by helping you to draw up your own step-by-step plan, and they may even be able to reward you for your achievements. Getting your child involved in this way can be good for a number of reasons: (i) it shows your child the strategies you are using to overcome your fear; (ii) it puts your child in a position of control and being the 'expert'; (iii) having someone to push you along will help your motivation; and (iv) it will make it all more fun!

Here's an example of the step-by-step plan that Layla and her mum came up with to overcome Mum's fear of cats:

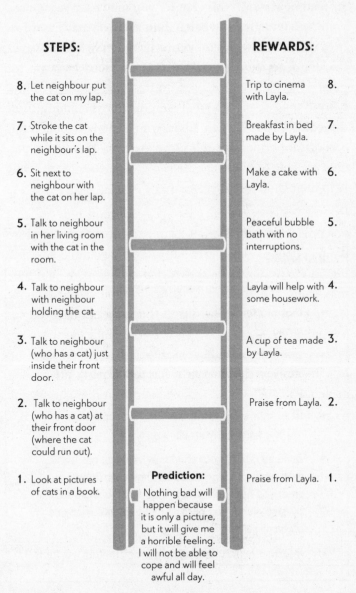

**STEPS:**

**8.** Let neighbour put the cat on my lap.

**7.** Stroke the cat while it sits on the neighbour's lap.

**6.** Sit next to neighbour with the cat on her lap.

**5.** Talk to neighbour in her living room with the cat in the room.

**4.** Talk to neighbour with neighbour holding the cat.

**3.** Talk to neighbour (who has a cat) just inside their front door.

**2.** Talk to neighbour (who has a cat) at their front door (where the cat could run out).

**1.** Look at pictures of cats in a book.

**REWARDS:**

Trip to cinema with Layla.    **8.**

Breakfast in bed made by Layla.    **7.**

Make a cake with Layla.    **6.**

Peaceful bubble bath with no interruptions.    **5.**

Layla will help with some housework.    **4.**

A cup of tea made by Layla.    **3.**

Praise from Layla.    **2.**

Praise from Layla.    **1.**

**Prediction:**
Nothing bad will happen because it is only a picture, but it will give me a horrible feeling. I will not be able to cope and will feel awful all day.

## If this isn't enough

By reading through this chapter you may have recognised your own thoughts and behaviours and you may have now tried out the strategies for yourself. You may feel, however, that the fears or worries that you are faced with are too great to tackle on your own. In this case you may find it helpful to seek professional support in overcoming these difficulties. Your GP can advise you on how to obtain this sort of support locally. It is our experience that where parents are able to overcome their own anxieties it can really help their child face their fears.

---

**Key points**

- Notice your worries about your child

- Look out for anxious signals or messages you may be giving

- Watch out for ways in which your own anxiety might stop your child from getting opportunities to face their fears

- If you can, work towards overcoming your own anxieties and get your child involved

- Demonstrate to your child how you deal positively with fears and worries by setting goals, finding out what you need to learn, testing fears (using a step-by-step plan if you need to build up gradually) and problem-solving

- If further help is needed, do not be afraid to ask for it

---

# 15

# Some final words on the guide: Keeping it going

We hope that you are now feeling more confident about applying the strategies we have discussed in the previous chapters. Now it is just a case of keeping going! As you can see from the gradual approach that we take to facing fears, the problems experienced with fears and worries are unlikely to go away overnight. It takes perseverance to keep working towards your child's goals. In our clinic we typically work with parents for a period of about two months. In that time, we would expect there to be noticeable changes, but we would not necessarily expect goals to always have been fully reached. If they have, then there are often new goals to strive for. It is rarely the end of the work. Within that period of time, however, we find that families have normally had a good chance to put their new skills into practice and they often feel confident that they no longer need our help and can continue working on their goals as a family.

From then on, we encourage families to keep practising the skills that they have learned, as this is the best way to keep progress going. Indeed, when we meet families a month or a year later we typically find that children have continued to achieve great things over that time.

## When progress is slow

At times it may feel as if you are not making progress, so at these times it is important to return to your early notes and review how much progress has been made with the goals that you set (Chapter 7). You may be pleasantly surprised by the progress that has been made. However, if progress is slow, you may need to review your goals to make sure that they still apply and are 'SMART'. In addition, it is likely that some skills we have described worked particularly well with your child, whereas they may have taken to others less well. It will be useful to remember which things particularly seemed to help your child for those times in the future when you want to make a concerted effort to help him or her face a particular fear.

## What has helped your child?

In the box on page 221, make a note of the things that you have found particularly helped your child to overcome anxiety, so that you can refer back to this in the future.

## Problems you may face

The table on page 224 describes some specific problems that parents have told us they found as they tried to overcome their child's fears and worries. We urge you not to be put off by these problems, but to use the skills that you and your child have been practising with this book to overcome them. So, rather than telling you what to do we have made some suggestions for strategies you might be able to use to find your own solution (just as we have been encouraging you to do when helping your child). This way you are putting into practice the skills you have learned and also coming up with solutions that are going to suit you.

| THINGS I HAVE DONE THAT HAVE BEEN HELPFUL FOR REDUCING MY CHILD'S ANXIETY |
|---|
|  |
|  |
|  |
|  |
|  |
|  |
|  |
|  |
|  |

One common problem that arises is when two parents have different approaches to the management of their child's anxious feelings and behaviours. This was the case for Layla's parents. They had separated a few years earlier but tried to get along with each other for their daughter's sake, and they both found it difficult. One thing they disagreed about was Layla's anxiety. Layla's dad felt that her mum mollycoddled her and that Layla should just be told to get on with it. Her mum, however, felt that her dad was too strict and did not show Layla enough understanding. The problem was made worse by the fact that the more Layla's mum tried to be sympathetic and supportive the more the dad thought she was being mollycoddled – making him more strict with Layla. And the firmer he was, the more Layla's mum wanted to protect her.

As the main carer, Layla's mum embarked on this programme to overcome Layla's anxiety, but the programme stalled when Layla went to visit her dad. Layla's mum was concerned that she and her ex-husband had such different ideas about how to manage their daughter's anxiety that they were not being consistent, and that because there were gaps of a week at a time when nothing was happening towards overcoming Layla's anxiety, they were making slow progress. Her mum sat down with a problem-solving chart to try to work out a solution to this problem. What she came up with is shown on page 226.

## Keep it going

If things have been going well and your child has made great progress, it will be tempting to stop practising the techniques and sit back and reap the rewards of your hard work! You must, however, keep on your toes and be on the lookout for opportunities to continue using the strategies. The more familiar your child is with the strategies, the more they will become your child's habitual way of dealing with problems. They will also be better prepared to use the strategies for dealing with any problems that they face throughout life and for avoiding becoming highly anxious in the future.

When Sarah was able to hold a spider in her hand she and her parents had got further than they'd imagined they would. That did not stop them continuing to use their new skills, however. Whenever any situation came up in the future that worried Sarah they continued to help her test out her anxious expectations by facing her fears (rather than avoiding them) or problem-solve to find a solution. They noticed that with time Sarah seemed to be able to learn new things about her anxious expectations without their support. Where there was a genuine problem, rather than letting it cause her a great deal of worry, she focused on what she needed to do to sort out the problem. As her life progressed she became a resourceful and resilient young woman.

## COMMON PROBLEMS THAT PARENTS FACE IN OVERCOMING THEIR CHILD'S FEARS, WORRIES AND ANXIETY

| PROBLEM | TIPS FOR FINDING A SOLUTION |
|---|---|
| Practical problems | |
| I don't have enough time to do the exercises. | Try 'problem-solving' (Chapter 11). |
| It's quicker (easier) to just do something for my child, rather than trying to get her to do it herself. | Is this really true when you think about it in the long term as well as the short term? |
| I don't know when to push my child. Is he anxious or is he not interested? | Is there a strategy that you could use whatever the reason (such as rewards)? |
| Other family members have different ideas about what is the right thing to do. | Try 'problem-solving'. Could you share other chapters in this book with your family? |
| When my child 'acts up' I don't know if this is because she is upset or being difficult. | Again, is there a strategy that you could use whatever the reason (such as rewards)? Also see Chapter 10 on overcoming difficult behaviour. |
| I'm not there at the times that my child worries about. | Try 'problem-solving'. |
| It seems unfair to my other children to be rewarding one child for doing things that they do all the time. | Try 'problem-solving'. Is there anything your other children would benefit from being rewarded for? |

| | |
|---|---|
| We know what our child needs to do to overcome his fears, but those situations just don't happen very often in everyday life. | Try 'problem-solving'. Also think about creating the right opportunities. |

| Personal problems | |
|---|---|
| I find it hard to keep motivated to keep 'pushing' my child. | See Chapter 14 on managing your own anxiety. Try 'problem-solving'. |
| I can't help worrying about how my child will be able to manage if I give them a push. | What is it that worries you? How could you put your anxious thoughts to the test? |
| It's hard to push my child to do something, when other members of the family have the same problem and aren't doing anything about it. | Try 'problem-solving'. |

## LAYLA'S MUM'S PROBLEM-SOLVING

| What is the problem? | List all the possible solutions | What would happen if I chose this solution? (In the short term? In the long term? To my anxiety in the future?) | Is this plan doable? Yes/No | How good is this plan Rate 0–10? | What happened? |
|---|---|---|---|---|---|
| Layla's dad and I handle Layla's anxiety differently, so the programme is not being followed consistently | 1. Carry on as I am | Nothing would change. I'd carry on as I am. I may make some progress, but it would be much slower than if we were both on board. | Yes | 5 | |

| | | | |
|---|---|---|---|
| 2. Talk to Layla's dad about what I have been doing and ask him to do the same. | He would think I am criticising him. We would get into an argument. Unlikely much would change. | Yes | 2 |
| 3. Share what I have been reading with Layla's dad and show him the records I have kept of what I have done so far. | He could take it away and read it. Might be less likely to feel criticised. If he sees progress from what I have done so far, he might be more likely to think it is worth a try. | Yes | 8 |

# Future goals

Have a think now about what you feel it is important for you and your child to continue to work on. Make a note of this in the box below so that you can refer back to this in the future to see what progress you have made in working towards those goals.

| THINGS FOR ME AND MY CHILD TO CONTINUE TO WORK ON |
| --- |
| _____ |
| _____ |
| _____ |
| _____ |
| _____ |
| _____ |
| _____ |
| _____ |
| _____ |
| _____ |
| _____ |

Muhammed met his goal of sleeping in his bedroom on his own, but once he had achieved that it became clear to his parents that, because of his fears about separation, there were still certain things he would not do. For example, Muhammed had been invited to a sleepover party but had insisted that his parents pick him up before everyone went to sleep. His parents also longed for a night out together, yet had never been able to get a babysitter for Muhammed as he found the idea terrifying. Muhammed's parents generated the following list of goals to continue to work on.

---

**Things for us to continue to work on with Muhammed**

1.  Muhammed to stay at home with a babysitter.

2.  Muhammed to go on day trip with school without parents.

3.  Muhammed to stay away from home overnight (with a friend/grandparents).

4.  Muhammed to go to scout camp.

---

# Reward yourself!

Finally, we would like you to take this opportunity to stop and think about the achievements that you and your child have made. Throughout the programme you will have been rewarding your child for their efforts and we hope that you will continue to do so. At this point though, you should also acknowledge that if your child has made progress then it has been down to the help that you have been giving them. Although we are sure that your child's progress is a reward in itself, perhaps the time has come to reward yourself for all the work that you have put in to make this happen. Have a nice meal or a long bath, arrange a night out, get together with a friend. Whatever you do, just be sure to mark the occasion and give yourself the credit that you deserve for helping your child overcome their fears and worries.

Ben's parents took this on board. They had really struggled to help him overcome his fear of going upstairs alone. One of the things that they found most difficult, but most helpful, was making the time to talk to Ben about his fears about the monster and taking his concerns seriously. It was surprisingly hard to not just say, 'Don't be silly, Ben. There is no monster!' They persevered, however, and made an effort to take their time and help Ben work out for himself that the monster in the film was not a real danger to him. Their efforts paid off, and within a month Ben had reached the top of his step-by-step plan and was able to play happily upstairs, even when no one else was within hearing distance. To reward him for all his hard work, Ben received his ultimate reward of a trip to a theme park. Ben's parents could see the hard work that Ben had put in, but they also had to acknowledge that nothing would have changed if they had not worked so hard to give Ben the support and encouragement he needed. So, they asked a relative to come round, and Ben's parents treated themselves to a well-deserved night out!

---

**Key points**

- Keep practising the skills you have learned

- Keep working towards new goals

- Use these skills to overcome problems along the way

- Reward yourself for the work that you have done and the progress you have made. Well done!

---

# PART III

◇◇◇◇◇◇◇◇◇◇◇◇

# Addressing
# Particular Needs

# 16

# Using this book with younger children

This book describes an approach to overcoming anxiety that we have tested out and have found to be useful with children of primary school age (from 5 to 12 years). In our studies we have found that children across this age range do equally well from this approach. However, if your child is at the younger end then some of the strategies that we suggest might seem a bit tricky. If your child is about seven years of age or younger we suggest that you read this chapter after you have read through Part Two, but before you actually start to embark on the programme. This will give you some tips on ways to make the most of the programme with a younger child.

## How much anxiety is normal in younger children?

It is common for young children to get anxious about all kinds of things. It is part of growing up and learning about the world. For example, toddlers are often startled by loud noises whereas 4- and 5-year-olds are often afraid of monsters or the dark. This is normal, and it is likely that your child will simply grow out of these fears. The strategies in this chapter will, however, be useful to prevent these fears becoming a problem. This chapter will also be helpful to address any fears that may have been typical for your child's age in the past, but which have persisted while other children have grown out of them. It will also, of course, help if a fear or worry is getting in your child's way (for example, stopping them doing things that they would enjoy doing).

## What do I need to do differently with younger children?

In Part Two we have described a whole range of strategies that you can use to help your child overcome anxiety. We will now discuss which of these strategies work best with younger children and talk about ways in which you can adapt these ideas to help a young child to use them. The main thing to emphasise is that with younger children, talking in detail about the problem may be difficult (and not necessarily helpful), so it will be important to keep focused on how your child can learn what they need to learn through doing. Your main job will be working out what your child needs to have a go at, what opportunities you will need to create, and how you can encourage your child to 'have a go' to make new discoveries that enable them to overcome their anxiety.

Think about how you can do new things in a way that will be fun for your child. For example, it has been shown that children who are fearful of speaking out loud to unfamiliar people can do very well by gradually building up the sounds they make in front of others using fun apps (such as blowing out onscreen flames or talking into voice-changer apps). It seems that playing fun games that enable children to have a go at things they feel worried about can make it easier for them to give new things a try and to discover that doing these things was not as bad as they had predicted. Think about how you can make facing fears feel like a game, for example can it be done like a game of 'dare' where you take turns doing (gentle) challenges?

## What does my child need to learn?

We talked in Chapter 8 about helping your child to spot their anxious expectations. With younger children you will need to ask simple questions, using simple language, such as 'What do you think is going to happen?' Young children often find it easier to describe something happening to someone else rather than themselves so, for example, talk to your child or make up a story about a friend or well-known character entering a situation that would frighten your child, and see what your child says will happen. For example, do they think he or she will get hurt, or that someone else will get hurt? Or that someone will get lost or taken away? You could also do this as part of a role-play game, using toy characters or puppets. Sometimes younger children will find it hard to articulate an anxious expectation other than predicting that they will get really upset. In fact, this might be the main outcome that they fear and wish to avoid. As we describe on page 101 it is absolutely fine to work with that expectation. It may be that they won't get as upset as predicted or it may be that your child gets to learn that even if they do get upset that's OK in the end.

## Encouraging independence and 'having a go'

Younger children will obviously be reliant on you or others for your support in many areas of their lives – this is completely normal. But can you think about age-appropriate ways that they can start to do more simple, everyday tasks for themselves? Are there times when you automatically step in? For example, hanging your child's coat up when they come in the door, choosing clothes to wear? Could you encourage them to do this for themselves instead? If it would be helpful, talk to other parents about things that their child does or doesn't do for themselves to give you ideas of ways you can safely support your child to feel more in control of their environment by increasing their independence in day-to-day life.

In Chapter 9 we talked about how you can encourage your child to 'have a go' at things that make them anxious. Work hard to make these things fun. You should also make sure you give them lots of attention and praise when they are being brave, and try not to give too much attention when they are anxious. Young children (particularly anxious young children) are especially sensitive to the messages they receive from their parents, so this principle is particularly important. We know that if we praise or give attention to good behaviour (such as eating nicely at dinner), your child is more likely to do this again, whereas if we ignore difficult behaviour (such as a tantrum) this behaviour is less likely to happen again.

Children start to learn at an early age that their actions have consequences. At less than two years of age children recognise verbal praise and will behave in a way that is likely to attract it. Immediate rewards (such as stickers) will also act to reinforce positive behaviour from about three years of age, and from four years or so children will be able to alter their behaviour with the promise of slightly less immediate rewards (for example, using star charts to save up for a reward). So, we need to be paying attention to children's positive and 'have a go' behaviour from an early age and responding to it with clear praise.

Your child is now learning that when they 'have a go' good things happen. It is also important that they learn that when they are not able to 'have a go' *nothing bad happens*, but, at the same time, *nothing good happens*. When your child refuses to 'have a go' or becomes anxious or distressed it would be wrong to ignore them completely, but what you can do is ignore the *fear* and the *anxious behaviour*. The simplest way to do this is to distract your child to help get their mind off the fear, but without removing them from the situation (and encouraging avoidance). So, for example, if your child becomes nervous as they approach the school playground, change the conversation to point out something happening in the distance ('Wow, what is that cat doing?'), talk about something good that will be happening today, or what they would like to do after school. By using this strategy, you are not giving attention to your child's fear and they are helped to cope with the fear. They also start to discover that just because something seems scary at first it doesn't mean they can't deal with it, and they may even end up enjoying it!

## Overcoming fears and worries step by step

Just as with older children, a step-by-step plan is a useful way to help your child gradually build up the number of things they can 'have a go' at to test their anxious predictions.

Once again, where we previously encouraged you to help your child to devise the step-by-step plan themselves, with younger children you will have to take a more active role and create the plan with or for your child. As before, identify an ultimate goal and work out a series of gradual steps to build up to this goal. Offer clear rewards that you know will motivate your child to have a go at each step. If they are reluctant to have a go then the step is too big and will need breaking down. An example of a step-by- step plan for a younger child, Joe (aged 5 years) is on page 241.

## Everyday life

The strategies described in this chapter will help your child to put different predictions to the test, to 'have a go' and not let fear get in the way in order to help them recognise that there are different ways of thinking about situations. These can be thought of as good skills for life.

# Joe's step-by-step plan

| STEPS: | PREDICTION: | REWARDS: |
|---|---|---|

**Ultimate goal**
To stroke the dog when Granddad is not holding her.

**Ultimate reward**
A day trip to the beach.

**7.** To stroke the dog on her head while Granddad holds her.

Choose a movie to watch    **7.**

**6.** To touch the dog while Granddad holds her.

Have a friend round for tea.    **6.**

**5.** To stay in the living room while Granddad takes the dog off the lead and holds her.

Buy a sweet on the way home.    **5.**

**4.** To go for a walk round the block with Granddad, taking the dog on the lead.

Buy a comic on the way home.    **4.**

**3.** To stay in the living room when Granddad brings the dog in on a lead.

Go to the park on the way home.    **3.**

**2.** To go into Granddad's living room when the dog is in the kitchen.

Play with Granddad's toy cars.    **2.**

**Prediction:**
The dog will bark, and it will bark really loud. It will be really scary, and I will be really scared. The dog might find a way in.

**1.** To go in to Granddad's house when the dog is in the garden.

A sweet from Granddad's tin.    **1.**

## Tips for successful rewards with younger children

- Make sure your child understands what they will get as a reward if they can 'have a go' at a step on the plan ('If you come into the living room with Tessie, we'll go to the park on the way home').

- Be clear what they are getting the reward for ('Well done, because you managed to say hello to the lady at the checkout, we'll go and make the cakes now').

- Praise your child every time they do each step, not just once. Continue to give rewards if your child still feels fearful about doing trying the step.

- Give your child the reward immediately after they have completed the step, or as soon as possible afterwards (if necessary, buy the reward beforehand so you have it ready to give to your child).

- With younger children, rewards that involve *doing* things with you can be as or more meaningful than material rewards (that is, buying things).

- Give your child lots of praise for completing the step ('Well done for having your friend round, you were really brave, and Daddy is very proud of you').

Take opportunities to encourage your child to learn these principles during everyday life and make them a part of your lifestyle. They will stand your child in good stead for dealing with problems that they will encounter long into the future.

## Key points

- Help your child to describe what they think will happen in situations they are scared of

- Encourage 'have a go' behaviour with praise and rewards to help your child test anxious predictions

- Have fun – the main thing is to encourage your child to 'have a go'

- Use a step-by-step plan to face fears gradually

- Take opportunities to practise these strategies in everyday life

# 17

# Using this book with older children and teenagers

This book describes an approach to overcoming anxiety that we have tested out and have found to be useful with children of primary school age (from 5 to 12 years). We have not tested this approach with older children and teenagers, but many of the principles that we have described in this book are commonly used with children in this age group who are anxious, so you may find them useful if you are looking to help an adolescent with fears or worries.

## How can I help my older child or teenager overcome anxiety?

Teenagers may be particularly likely to be sensitive to what they think other people are thinking about them and may also be sensitive to feeling that parents and carers are overly interfering in their lives as they strive for independence. So, one of the biggest challenges you will face is talking to your adolescent in a way that lets them feel that you are genuinely interested in their point of view and take this seriously. If you can successfully show your adolescent that you understand their anxiety problems, then you are well on your way to helping overcome them. As we discussed at the beginning of Part Two, it is not just *what* you say and do that will be important, but also *how* you say or do it. For your teenager to work with you, you need to show that you understand and accept what they are worried about. You are not criticising or judging them; however, you do recognise that this worry is getting in the way and something needs to be done about it.

## Does your older child or teenager want to change?

Although you may view your teenager's worries as being problematic, it is possible that they do not feel the same way. For your teenager to make progress they will need to want to make changes. Telling your child that he or she *has* to do the things in this book will lead to more reluctance on their part. Instead, listen to your teenager and show that you understand their point of view. Ask about their goals and whether fears or worries will create any difficulties in achieving them. In the end, the choice is your child's, but your job is to help them make an *informed* choice.

Here is an example of a conversation between Jill, a teenager who worried excessively about exams, and her dad.

> Dad:   *Jill, I've bought this book about helping young people to overcome their fears because I thought*

it might help you with worries about exams.
From reading it I can see I would need you to be
working with me for it to work. How do you feel
about that?

Jill: I don't need to work on anything. I'm fine how I
am.

Dad Well, if you are fine how you are then that's OK.
I suppose it doesn't necessarily get in your way
that much, does it?

Jill: No. I only worry when I have an important test
or exams are coming up.

Dad: Yes, and I guess that's not very often. Do you
think it might be more of a problem this year
though?

Jill: Not really. I guess when the exams get closer and
when I have mocks I might get more anxious.

Dad: Yes, would you like to feel less anxious around
exam time?

Jill: Maybe.

Dad This might seem like a big question, but I was
wondering – what do you imagine things being

> like in two years or five years' time when you are
> doing your A levels or even university exams if
> you go there?

Jill: I don't know. I hope I'd be OK with them by
then.

Dad: Do you think your worries about exams might
get in the way of doing those exams or make
things really miserable for you?

Jill: I don't think so...maybe, I suppose as you have
exams every year at uni I think.

Dad: So it sounds like your worries about exams
aren't a huge problem for you right now, but you
might feel happier if it was sorted out as things
might get harder for you this year and in sixth
form. I guess we've got two options: to stay the
same or to try to overcome the fear. It really is up
to you, but as long as you know I'd like to help if
you decide you want to go for it. OK?

## What do I need to do differently with my older child?

If your child has made the choice to have a go at overcoming their fears or worries, you are over halfway there. The strategies that we have discussed in Part Two are often used with adolescents. We will now highlight some points to consider when using these strategies with an older child or teenager.

## Giving adolescents more control

The main difference in helping older children to overcome their anxiety is that they need to be put in a position of greater control over the strategies that they use. Although they still need your support and guidance, they will be much more capable of carrying out some of the strategies independently, and, in fact, they are likely to want to do them independently, rather than have you tell them what to do! It is really important to remember this. If you insist on taking charge, your teenager is likely to lose interest and refuse to participate at all. You may also want to encourage them to get their friends involved, or other adults that they know well. Although parents want to help, sometimes your teenager will welcome help from others more than from you.

A good starting point might be to get your teenager to read this book, or parts of it that seem most relevant, to decide whether they think it's worth a try. Immediately, you are giving them more control, rather than telling them what to do. Then, perhaps you can ask them which goal they want to set first, which one makes most sense and how they would like you to help. In this way, you are allowing your teenager to take the lead. It is also worth asking who else they think might be able to help them have a go at some of the tasks in this book. Are there friends or other adults who could provide a bit of support?

## What does my teen need to learn?

In Chapter 8 we talked about how you, as a parent, could try to find out what your child's anxious expectations are so that you can help your child to test them out by trying new things. With adolescents, you can use the same process, but you will need to pay attention to how much involvement your child wants you to have, and how much of your involvement your child needs. For example, might they need your help to create the right opportunities? Or might your involvement prevent them from really learning something new (i.e. is relying on your help a 'safety behaviour'?). You don't want your teenager to feel as if they are now going it alone, however, so at the least, review the record sheets with them every few days or even once a week, and congratulate them on how well they are working to overcome fears and worries.

## Encouraging independence

Chapter 9 was about encouraging your child to be independent and to 'have a go'. The teenage years are a critical time when young people move from dependence to independence. They will naturally be expected to be independent in many ways – for example, making their own way to school. The more your child feels 'in control' of his or her world, the easier it will be.

As always, it is important not to throw your child in at the deep end, as you want to help them feel in control, not cause panic. Be clear with your child what you expect them to be responsible for, gradually increasing the things that they are in control of (e.g. making packed lunch, packing school bag, waking self up in the morning). While teenagers need opportunities for independence they still need our support to learn new skills and our help to make choices. This can be a tricky balancing act for parents who also need to adjust to their new role as 'support crew'.

## Praise and rewards

Another key thing we discussed in Chapter 9 was praise and rewards. Although the concept of rewards may seem quite childish it can still be a powerful motivator with older children and adolescents. Its success depends on the choice of rewards. Of course, you must agree to the rewards before your teenager starts to face their fears, so that they do not do so thinking that they will achieve something unrealistic, but it must be your teenager who makes the choice, as only they will know what will motivate them to face their fears. In contrast to younger children, doing things with you may be less of a motivator for some teenagers – but coming up with ways that you can facilitate activities that they can do with friends will provide good alternatives to material and financial rewards.

## *Using a step-by-step plan with an adolescent*

Chapter 10 described how to make a step-by-step plan to help your child gradually test out his or her anxious predictions. A step-by-step plan can be a useful tool for children of any age, and indeed adults too, particularly when the person has mixed feelings about testing out their fears. Doing this gradually can help them to notice that they can cope with a bit of a challenge and that good things might come of it. With an adolescent, you do not necessarily need to call it a step-by-step plan – you can refer to it as a ladder or hierarchy or whatever makes most sense to them – but the principle remains the same. Your adolescent needs to stop avoiding situations that make them anxious but instead try out situations that allow them to test out anxious predictions. The step-by-step plan gives a clear plan of action with lots of small goals leading to the ultimate goal, with rewards along the way to both motivate and acknowledge his or her efforts.

## *Problem-solving skills*

In Chapter 11 we talked about how you can help your child to solve problems. The problem-solving strategies we discussed may be particularly useful for older children. Adolescence is a time when your child will be becoming more independent, and one part of this process is for them to be able to start dealing with tricky situations on their own. The problem-solving steps we described in Chapter 11 are a good way of starting to help them do just this, with your support.

Initially, you will need to teach your child how to problem-solve, by working through the steps together. However, once they have got the hang of these, they can start to do it more independently. Your child should be able to come up with a list of possible solutions and to be able to rate them in terms of how good they are and how doable. They may want to check with you whether their preferred solution is a good one, and it's important that you remember to ask how they got on with putting the chosen solution into action.

---

### Key points

- Show genuine interest in your older child or teenager's thoughts. Maintain a non-judgmental manner

- Help your teenager make an informed choice about whether to try to overcome their fears or worries

- Follow the steps described in Part Two, but allow your child to be in control as much as possible

# 18

# Sleep problems

Problems at night-time are extremely common among anxious children. Sometimes it's difficult for children to settle to sleep by themselves; they may worry excessively at bedtime – sometimes about not being able to get to sleep. As a result, your child may like you to stay with them as they go to sleep, keep coming out of bed to check in with you, or they may sleep in your bed with you. Your child may also wake frequently during the night and find it very hard to get back to sleep and feel the need to come and seek you out during the night.

This is all exhausting for parents. It can mean that you are getting very little time to yourself or for you and your partner to be together, and it can mean you are functioning on minimal (and broken) sleep. As all parents know from having young babies, this can be very draining. When you are tired it is extremely difficult to be the patient person that you might otherwise be, and you are likely to, at times, feel resentful of this time that your child is demanding when you just need some time to yourself.

At other times parents may simply feel resigned to the fact that this is just how things are going to be. If it is not causing anyone a problem now, then that may be absolutely fine. If, for example, you are all getting enough sleep, it is not affecting relationships within the family, and it is not stopping your child doing things that other children their age are doing (such as going to sleepovers and having friends to stay). You do need to think carefully, however, about how much longer the current situation will be acceptable. Will you still be happy about things being the same when your child is eight? Ten? Starting secondary school? Starting work? The point we are making is that if your child is having night-time difficulties this situation should not be accepted, as permanent change can be made.

## Is good sleep being promoted?

First and foremost, you need to be certain that the environment is right for your child to be able to go to sleep. Run through the simple checklist on page 255.

## Sleep Checklist

| | |
|---|---|
| Is your child's bedroom too hot? | Turn the heaters down. Open windows slightly. Use a fan. |
| Is your child's bedroom too cold? | Turn the heaters up. Add a blanket. |
| Is your child's bed uncomfortable? | Change the mattress/bed or can you put another layer under the sheet? Change the bedding. |
| Is your child's room too light? | Hang a towel over the curtain or invest in blackout blinds. If your child likes a light on at night-time, ensure it is a night light with a low-wattage bulb. |
| Is your child's room too dark? | Use a night-light. |
| Is your child's room too noisy? | The solution depends on the source of the noise. Can you ask people to be quieter? Can the room be insulated at all (such as hanging a heavy towel over the window)? |
| Are there distractions keeping your child awake (such as screens, computer games)? | Restrict their use or remove them! |
| Is your child tired enough? | Cut down/cut out daytime naps if your child has them. Wake your child earlier. |
| | Build an outdoor activity into your early-evening routine (but not too near to bedtime, so there's plenty of time to wind down). There is good evidence that exercise and fitness are linked to sleep quality. |

| | |
|---|---|
| Is your child 'charged up' at bedtime (from playing computer games, watching screens, for example)? | Restrict these stimulating activities to earlier in the day. Make sure your child does not use a screen or electronic device in the hour leading up to bedtime. |
| Is your child drinking a lot before bed? | Cut down/cut out drinks in the hour before bedtime. Make sure your child visits the toilet before bed. |
| Is your child eating/drinking caffeine? | Cut down/cut out caffeinated drinks/foods (such as cola, chocolate) in the hours before bedtime. |
| Does your child not know when to go to bed? | Make sure your child has a regular bedtime routine. Do the same things in the same order each night and make sure your child goes to bed at roughly the same time each night |

## Night-time fears

Having established an environment that is going to help (not hinder) your child's sleep, the focus now turns to your child. The main reasons for sleep problems in anxious children are:

1. Fear of being alone or separated from a loved one.

2. Uncontrollable worry or specific worries about not sleeping

In order to know exactly how best to approach your child's night-time fears and worries you need to work through the steps described in Part Two.

1.  Decide on your goals and your child's goals for their anxiety at bedtime.

2.  Work out what your child's anxious expectations are at bedtime and what they need to learn to overcome their fears.

3.  Encourage, praise and rewards your child's brave behaviour and attempts to overcome this fear.

4.  Develop a step-by-step plan and/or use one-off experiments so your child can gather new information about their anxious expectations.

5.  Use problem-solving to address bedtime related problems.

## What does my child need to learn?

Use the questions in Chapter 8 to help you find out what your child's anxious expectations are about bedtime (see box, page 90). Some children worry about something bad happening at night time, such as someone breaking into their home or a house fire – and for many children they find the idea of being the only one awake if this happens particularly frightening. For this reason, they may want to sleep with you close by and fear being alone or away from you. For other children, their worries relate to not being able to sleep or to get to sleep; they might expect that they will not do well at school the next day if they are tired or won't perform well in a football match or sporting activity, or will simply just be awake all night. The next step is to figure out what your child then needs to learn to overcome their fear (see Chapter 8, pages 102–104). For a child who is fearful of sleeping alone, they will probably need to learn that they can actually cope if they sleep alone and that it is unlikely that something bad will happen. Similarly, for a child who is worried about the consequences of not sleeping, it might be helpful to learn that they can in fact cope pretty well at school after a bad night's sleep, or that they actually always get to sleep reasonably quickly and get enough sleep.

## A step-by-step approach to helping your child sleep alone

The next step is to help your child gather new information about their anxious expectations to help them overcome their fear. When it comes to night-time, we want to give your child the opportunity to learn that, for example, they can be alone and can cope. By adopting a step-by-step approach your child will not be put straight into a very anxiety-provoking situation but will instead gradually build up what they are able to do. In order to draw up a step-by-step plan with your child, read through Chapter 10 again carefully. A fairly typical example of this in relation to fear of sleeping alone is shown on page 259 in Muhammed's step-by-step plan.

## Muhammed's step-by-step plan

### STEPS:

**Ultimate goal**

To sleep on my own in my own room all night, every night for a week.

**6.** To sleep in my room alone with one of my parents coming to check on me every half-hour until I am asleep, for a week.

**5.** To sleep in my room alone with one of my parents coming to check on me every 20 minutes until I am asleep, for a week.

**4.** To sleep in my room alone with one of my parents coming to check on me every 10 minutes until I am asleep, for two nights in a row.

**3.** To sleep in my room alone with one of my parents upstairs while I settle to sleep.

**2.** To sleep in my room all night with my cousin staying over with me.

**1.** To sleep in my room all night with Dad in the same room on the camp bed.

**Prediction:**

No one will come in when Dad is there. But if Dad needs to go to the toilet in the night a bad man might come in and get me when he is gone.

### REWARDS:

**Ultimate reward**

Have four friends over for a sleepover.

A trip to the cinema.    **6.**

A day out with my **5.** family.

Watch a film and **4.** stay up a bit later than usual.

Dad will play a **3.** board game with me.

My favourite **2.** breakfast in the morning.

Praise from Mum **1.** and Dad.

One thing to remember in setting up a step-by-step plan is that your child cannot make themselves actually fall asleep at a particular time. A step like 'be asleep within 10 minutes' is guaranteed to fail and is simply going to put more pressure on your child (making it harder for him or her to drop off to sleep). Your child can, however, learn to be comfortable in their room alone and learn to settle down to sleep. Some children take longer than others to settle down, and it can become very boring for them lying in their bed not being able to fall asleep. Are there gentle activities that you would be happy for your child to do as they calm down for sleep, such as reading or listening to audiobooks? Your child may also be reluctant to take the step of being alone in the bedroom. For this reason, if your child is not sleeping in their own room we recommend getting them back in there and getting used to that environment again straight away. Using your step-by-step plan, you can then move yourself away from your child, rather than vice versa. So, for example, rather than gradually moving your child out of your room, start with you in your child's room, too, and gradually move yourself away night by night (by sleeping in the room one night, then the following night you would move your bed/mattress nearer to the door. The next night you would be outside the room but not far away, and so on). Or if you don't need to be so close by at the start of the step plan, encourage your child to sleep alone but with you checking on them every few minutes until they are asleep. Gradually lengthen the period between visits as your child progresses.

Night-time can be a time when children feel particularly vulnerable, but if your child's fear of being alone is not specific to night-time you will need to build early steps in to your plan which allow them to get used to being alone in their room during the daytime. The essential thing to remember is that each step is taking you forward. Once your child can tolerate the step that you are working on then move forward.

One-off experiments can also be used (in addition to a step-by-step plan) to gather new information about a child's anxious expectations at bedtime, for example, fears about burglars. Here are two examples:

- When your child hears a worrying noise, help them to check the house to find out what the noise really is.

- Do a survey to find out how many people your child knows have actually been burgled and if they have been, how they coped.

Remember with each step or each experiment, be sure to get your child to make a prediction about what they expect will happen before they do it. Then review this with them afterwards to see what actually happened and what they have learned. Did it pan out as they expected or was it different? If it was different, how? What happened instead?

## Worry at bedtime

Most nights it takes us all a little while to fall asleep and this is a time when worries that have arisen during the day can pop into our heads and make it harder for us to get to sleep. If your child experiences uncontrollable worry generally, they are likely to worry an awful lot at bedtime and this may impact on their ability to get to sleep. In this case, the strategies described in Chapter 12 can be applied. In particular you will find it useful to set a 'worry time' that takes place at another time of day. If your child mentions worries at bedtime, allow these to be added to the worry list and agree to discuss them at the next 'worry time' but don't get drawn into a discussion when your child mentions them. Help your child to come up with ways of relaxing and focusing their mind on other things at bedtime. Distractions such as reading, listening to music or to an audio book often work well. You may need to devise a step-by-step plan that involves your child gradually becoming more independent in dealing with their worries at bedtime, for example, having steps that involve your child holding back on calling out but using strategies to distract themselves, and rewarding your child for coping with their worries independently.

Some children don't worry excessively during the day but have specific worries about bedtime and sleep. For example, some children worry that they won't be able to get to sleep, will lie awake all night, and that perhaps as a result, they will do badly at school or in a sports match the next day. In this situation, coming up with a step-by-step plan can be hard, as your child may not be avoiding anything in particular. Nevertheless, experiments can be used to gather new information to challenge their anxious expectations.

Here are some examples of one-off experiments for this type of worry:

- Stay up late before a football match. Ask friends and the coach how I performed.

- Go to bed an hour later than usual and see if I get into trouble at school the next day for not doing my work because I am too tired.

- Try and stay awake as long as I can and find out whether it is actually possible to stay awake all night or whether we always fall asleep eventually.

- Accept an invitation to the cinema on a school night and see what happens.

Some of these tasks might feel challenging for parents as it is understandably important that our children get a good night's sleep in general. Here we are asking you to hold off giving the sorts of messages that we all commonly give our children, such as 'you need to get to sleep or you'll feel terrible in the morning'. While these comments are very natural and normal, for a child who is highly anxious about not sleeping, they may feed in to a vicious cycle in which not sleeping leads to concerns about sleeping which make it harder to get to sleep!

# Using problem-solving with bedtime fears

Problem-solving (see Chapter 11) can be a really useful strategy for bedtime fears. Your child may need to find some ways of calming themselves at bedtime (without your help) and you can problem-solve how to do this with them and consider what is the best idea to try first. Another great use of problem-solving, as we described in Chapter 11, is to come up with a plan for your child's anxious expectation or worst fear, to give them a sense of control over what might happen. So if your child is worried about burglars, you could support them in problem-solving what to do if, albeit unlikely, a burglar did break in. Get your child to consider all possible things they and you could do and decide on the best one to try. That way, your child has a greater sense of control over this situation.

## Other sleep-related problems

### Nightmares

As well as being very common, nightmares can also be extremely frightening. Children may wake up in the night and feel too frightened to go back to sleep in case they have the nightmare again. Where possible, children should be offered comfort and returned to their own beds. Nightmares can relate to something frightening that the child has heard or experienced during the day. It is important to give your child an opportunity, during the daytime, to tell you about the nightmare so that you can help them overcome any fears or worries that appear to have been a trigger, using the general principles used in this book.

## Night terrors

Typically, night terrors occur within the first hours of falling asleep, when your child is in a deep sleep. The child appears to wake up suddenly (although is actually asleep) and looks terrified. They may be screaming, sweating and in a confused state, and have a rapid heartbeat. This can last varying amounts of time (such as 5–20 minutes). This is not related to a nightmare, and in the morning your child will generally not remember what happened. Night terrors can occur in people of any age but are most common in children aged 5–12 years. Although night terrors can be frightening for parents it is important to remember that they are not dangerous.

## THE FOLLOWING TIPS MAY HELP REDUCE THE ONSET OF NIGHT TERRORS

1.  Make sure your child is not overtired at bedtime. Move bedtime earlier if necessary.

2.  Change the pattern of your child's sleep cycle. Try waking up your child soon after they have gone to sleep (for example, within an hour) then letting them go back to sleep or waking them up just before the time they usually have a night terror.

3. Check with your GP if your child is on any medication that may be linked to night terrors.

4. Identify and work with your child to resolve any stress that your child is experiencing during the day.

## DURING A NIGHT TERROR

1. Stay calm. Don't try to reason with your child; just wait for the terror to pass.

2. Don't try to wake your child during the night terror, but it may help to wake your child up after the night terror has finished to reduce the chance of another one happening.

3. Sit with your child and do what you can to make them feel comfortable until it passes.

4. If your child is comfortable with this at the time, give them a gentle hug.

## *Sleepwalking*

Similar to a night terror, sleepwalking happens when your child is in a deep sleep and they will not remember it in the morning. Similar advice applies: don't try to wake your child, simply quietly steer them back to bed. If your child sleepwalks you need to consider whether your house is safe for night-time wanderings. You may need to put a stair gate at the top of the stairs to stop your child falling. Also, be sure to close windows and put away any potentially dangerous objects (or things that could be tripped over) before going to bed.

## Bedwetting

In children under the age of six years bedwetting is not unusual. In fact, it has been argued that bedwetting is not uncommon and should not necessarily be considered a 'problem' under the age of eight years, particularly among boys. If your child is below this age you may nonetheless find it helpful to take practical steps – for example, restricting drinks before bedtime, making sure your child visits the toilet before bed and, perhaps also, waking them at your bedtime to visit the toilet again. If you notice that there is an increase in bedwetting at times when your child feels anxious, you also need to be using Part Two of this book to overcome the daytime worries that your child is experiencing. You also need to work hard to make sure that the bedwetting does not become a source of anxiety in itself. In order to do this, it is important not to punish your child when they wet the bed. It may be difficult, but remain calm and try not to show your child your frustration. Instead be very matter of fact about the situation, change the bed and settle your child back to sleep quickly with little fuss. On the other hand, make sure you give your child a lot of praise every time they make it through a night without wetting.

If these steps have not been sufficient and your child is wetting the bed frequently, your GP may be able to refer your child to an enuresis (bedwetting) clinic.

**Key points**

- Take practical steps to create a good sleeping environment for your child

- Follow the steps in Part Two to tackle anxieties that relate to bedtime

- Draw up a step-by-step plan with your child with concrete rewards, or use one-off experiments to gather new information

- Use problem-solving to tackle bedtime-related problems or to come up with a plan for your child's worst fear

- Make time to discuss night-time worries during the day

# 19

# Overcoming difficult behaviour

Fears and worries can be quite overwhelming for children and young people. Some children will become very tearful in response to them, whereas others will show their reaction with a seemingly angry outburst or tantrum. Both responses reflect the difficulty the child is having keeping control of his or her emotions in the face of anxiety. When children have an outburst like this it can present a real dilemma for parents. On the one hand, the parent feels concerned about what has upset the child in this way. On the other hand, the child's behaviour seems naughty or defiant. In order to manage this behaviour, it will be necessary to get a good understanding of what has caused this reaction in your child and to help your child overcome the anxiety (using the principles in Part Two). Most commonly tantrums occur when a child is being asked to face their fears (see Chapter 10 – 'Troubleshooting', page 151). But your child also needs to learn that an aggressive outburst is not an acceptable way of expressing emotions. This chapter will give an overview of useful strategies that can be applied when an outburst occurs. Once things have calmed down you must then, however, take the opportunity to return to Part Two to identify and overcome any fears or worries that may have provoked this difficult behaviour.

## Attention and praise

We talked before about how positive behaviours can be built up by being on the lookout for them and giving them a lot of attention and praise. Often simply removing attention from negative behaviours and giving attention to other behaviours can make a big difference to how your child behaves. Changing where we focus our attention takes work, as much of the time we can't help noticing the 'bad' things while the 'good' things don't get noticed or are taken for granted. Think about a behaviour that you want your child to stop. Now think about what you would like your child to be doing instead. Let your child know that this is what you expect to see, be on the lookout for when it happens and make sure it gets praise and attention every time, while ignoring the behaviour you would like to stop.

In order to balance out time spent ignoring behaviours or potentially using time-out (see below), be sure to spend some one-on-one time with your child each day when you can focus on what he or she enjoys doing. This can often feel hard to fit in but is important for you both to make sure that you have some positive time together. Agree with your child what they would like to do (for example, play a game together, take the dog for a walk, make something, do some cooking, read to your child, play a computer game with them…). Ensure your child has your full attention and praise them at every opportunity while you are together.

## When behaviours can't be ignored

Sometimes your child may act in a way that cannot be ignored. This is the case when, as a result of their behaviour, someone could get hurt. It is essential that your child learns that this is both an inappropriate and an unhelpful way to solve problems. The following strategies are reserved only for behaviours that are completely unacceptable and cannot be ignored, and should be used sparingly. If the behaviour is simply disruptive but not actually hurting anyone, then stick with the strategy of ignoring the disruptive behaviour and being on the lookout for and praising the positive alternative. All of these strategies should also be carried out in as calm and controlled a manner as you can muster. What you are teaching your child here is self-control, so take the opportunity to set a good example of this to your child.

### Time out

Time out is based on the principle that children respond to attention. Calmly removing a child from the current situation completely and moving them to a situation where there is no attention available can be a powerful learning experience. Through time out children can learn (i) that certain behaviours do not gain attention from other people, and (ii) that by leaving the situation it can be easier to calm down, allowing us to sort problems out more effectively.

Time out can be implemented by either putting your child in (or asking them to go to) a different room or (for younger children) moving them to a different part of the room and withdrawing your attention. Before using time out, you need to be clear with your child about the situations in which you will be using it. The most common reason that time out doesn't work is that it gets overused (children get put in time out for any little thing) and it therefore becomes meaningless or even a game.

Talk to your child about what you will use time out for. It is also important to try to frame time out in a positive way; we often call it calming-down time. It is an opportunity for your child to (independently) learn to calm down when they are very cross. Your child also needs to know how long the time out will last. A general rule of thumb is one minute for each year of your child's life, but ultimately your child needs to stay in their 'calm place' until they are actually calm. At that point, go and find them, and praise them for being calm. If they don't want to leave their 'calm place' or simply ignore you, just leave them until they are ready to come out and re-engage.

Finally, when the time out is over, don't hold a grudge. In fact, try to do the opposite. Praise your child for calming down. The key to the success of time out is consistency. Remember to use it every time your child is aggressive or has an angry outburst that cannot be ignored. You will soon find, as they learn to calm down, and as attention for their undesirable behaviour is withdrawn, the outbursts reduce in frequency.

## *Managing your own emotions*

We talked earlier about what children learn from watching others (Chapter 9, page 125). The same applies to controlling angry emotions. If you or your partner is someone who finds it hard to control strong emotions, your child may have seen this, and it may have an effect on what they do when they get cross. It is therefore really important that you are able to show your child that you have ways to help you calm down when you get cross, too. In the same way that you are expecting your child to be able to leave the situation and to go and independently calm down, you will need to be able to do this, too. If this is very difficult for you, it might be something you want to practise or work on. If you feel that you have specific problems with anger management and this is causing difficulties for you or your family, it may be helpful to talk to your GP about getting some help for yourself.

## Actions and consequences

All children need to learn that their actions have consequences. Sometimes aggressive behaviour has 'natural consequences'. For example, if your child wrecks their bedroom they will have to either live in a messy bedroom or clear it up. This may be more difficult for you than for your child, but do let them experience the consequence of their behaviour, rather than trying to protect them (or you) from it.

You can also remove privileges or special items. To have an impact on your child you need to be removing meaningful items or privileges and you need to be removing them as an immediate consequence of your child's action. What you select will depend on your child's age and interests – for example, reducing the time your child is allowed on their electronic device; introducing earlier bedtimes for so many nights. Once again, these work much better, and are less punitive, if they are natural consequences of a child's behaviour. For example, if a child refuses to go to bed one night, and therefore doesn't settle until an hour later than usual, you may wish to introduce a consequence of going to bed half an hour earlier the following night. Similarly, if your child has a tantrum while doing their homework, and so doesn't get it done in time, you may wish to reduce their screen time, in order that the homework gets done the next day.

It is important to remember, however, that the best strategy is always to find ways to encourage your child to behave in a positive way (for example, giving praise or rewards whenever your child shows self-control in the face of angry emotions). Time out and removing privileges should be used sparingly.

## A final word about consistency

Your child is going to find it easier to learn what kinds of behaviours are acceptable if you are consistent in how you respond. If your child has two parents or caregivers, then sit down with the other adult and generate a list of behaviours that are causing problems for your child and how you are going to manage them. Your child is going to learn about how to behave in the face of anxiety most effectively if you are both responding in the same way.

**Key points**

- Always try to pay attention to your child's positive behaviours – praise and reward these

- Set a good example to your child of how you keep control of your angry emotions

- Limit use of time out to aggressive behaviour or angry outbursts

- Use natural consequences to address other difficult behaviours

- Be consistent in how you respond to your child's behaviour

# 20

# School-attendance difficulties

Children who have difficulties with anxiety can often feel nervous about attending school and it can sometimes lead to problems getting there at all.

## Why do children find going to school hard?

If children see things that happen at school as potentially threatening it is understandable that they will try to avoid these situations. There are various challenges involved in going to school, particularly for children who are anxious. For example, children need to separate from their main caregiver(s), answer questions in class, take tests, work in small groups, mix with other children at playtime and cope with what other children might say to them. Some children become anxious about going to school because they are being bullied, and we will talk about how to tackle this later.

# What should you do if your child refuses to go to school?

The first thing you need to do if your child refuses to go to school or gets very anxious or nervous before school is to try to find out what it is about school that is making them nervous.

Just as you have practised in relation to other fears and worries, the first step is to ask your child simple questions to try to get a good understanding of their anxious expectations (Chapter 8, page 90). Examples include: 'What worries you about going to school?', 'What do you think will happen if you do go to school?' or even 'What is the worst thing that might happen if you do go to school?' Your child may be reluctant to tell you why they are worried. Children are often concerned that their parent will storm into school to sort out the problem, making the child feel even more the centre of attention or making others think they are a 'telltale'. Persistence and trying different ways to ask your child about their fears and worries will probably be necessary, as will giving your child an assurance that you won't take any action without talking to them about it first.

If your child is not able to describe what is worrying them about going to school, you will need to talk with your child's teacher or someone else who knows them well. It is important to be open with your child that you are doing this, but also to let them know that you are doing this as discreetly as possible so that it does not lead to increased anxiety, for example about making bullies target them even more.

Once you have established what your child expects to happen at school, you need to make a plan of action in discussion with them. If your child has identified a particular problem that you both feel needs sorting out, use the strategies outlined in Chapter 11 to generate ways to solve the problem and evaluate them. A very common anxiety for children who have missed school either due to being ill or due to feeling very anxious is that their peers will judge them negatively for being away and may ask lots of questions or call them a 'skiver'. You can use problem-solving with your child to figure out how they can handle this tricky situation. As we have said before, if your child has a plan, they are likely to feel more in control and less anxious should the situation arise.

Here is some problem-solving, that Chloe, aged 12, did with her mum before starting to work on her step plan (page 279).

| What is the problem? | What could I do? | What would happen if I did this? | Rating (0–10) | |
|---|---|---|---|---|
| | | | How good would this be? | How easy would this be to do? |
| The boys are going to ask me questions about where I have been and will probably say I am a skiver | Tell them to mind their own business! | They might think I am being rude and annoy me even more or they might listen | 5 | 3 |
| | Be honest and tell them why I have been off school | I am scared they will tease me and won't understand | 4 | 3 |
| | Give them a brief answer and change the subject – say 'I have not been well but now I am much better' | They might accept this as I have given them an answer and hopefully they will get bored and move on to something else | 8 | 7 |
| | Say my grandma was ill | They might not believe me or ask why I had so much time off for that – there is a chance they might believe me and leave it there | 6 | 8 |

If you discover that your child expects something bad to happen at school or expects not to be able to cope, but that these expectations are in reality unlikely to happen, try to figure out what your child needs to learn to overcome their anxiety (Chapter 8, page 102), and devise a step plan with them to gather new information about their anxious expectations, just as Layla and her mother did (Chapter 10, page 136). Remember to ask your child to make a prediction or predictions about what they think will happen in each step, and then review this once they have completed it. What actually happened? Was it the same or different to their prediction? What have they learned?

It may be that your child is anxious about a whole range of situations at school and it is hard to know what to work on first. In these situations, we would recommend devising a step-by-step plan that is focused on getting your child into school consistently first. If your child is not attending school at all, start with them attending sessions at school that they find easiest and build up gradually. For example, some children will fear particular lessons, because of the teacher or other pupils in the class, while other children might find play/break time or lunchtime harder as it involves finding someone to play or hang out with.

Here is Chloe's step-by-step plan for getting back in to school:

## Chloe's step-by-step plan

**STEPS:**

**Ultimate goal**

Attend school every day for a week.

4. Attend all lessons until afternoon break.

3. Attend all lessons up to lunchtime.

2. Attend lessons up to lunchtime on Mondays, Wednesdays, and Fridays.

1. Attend morning lessons for one day.

**Prediction:**

Everyone will ask me lots of questions about where I have been. I won't know what to say. I will look stupid.

**REWARDS:**

**Ultimate reward**

Day trip to the seaside.

4. Have a friend round for sleepover.

3. Extra time on the games console.

2. Hot chocolate at the café.

1. Favourite food for tea.

## How to motivate your child

One of the biggest challenges for parents of children who struggle to attend school is how to motivate their child to 'have a go'. For many children, the obvious solution to their worries or anxious expectations is to just not go to school and they will rarely be really keen to work on a step plan like the one we have described above. Using rewards, as described in Chapter 9, page 119, can work really well. Agree a reward for each step that you can give to your child every time they complete that step. Think carefully about what rewards will motivate them, but also which rewards you will be able to offer more than once.

You also need to give your child a clear, positive message that they need to go to school and there will be positive aspects – for example, learning, seeing friends, doing sports or music etc. Sometimes it can be hard to give these messages; you might be concerned about how your child will manage in school, you might also be frustrated with how school have handled your child's anxiety, relationships or their learning needs. It will be important that you address these concerns with your child's school and have a plan in place so you can feel confident that your child's needs are being met. That way you can give your child a clear message that you understand their concerns, but action is being taken to support them in gradually overcoming their fears.

As well as avoiding the challenge of attending school, some children may also quite enjoy being at home! They may spend their time watching TV, on their computer playing games or doing other fun things. This will make school even less appealing and make them less motivated to overcome their fears about school. Addressing this situation takes work and supervision. The most important thing is to set some limits about what happens at home during school hours. For example, it is reasonable to limit your child to educational activities, including school work (which you can ask your child's teachers for), watching educational programmes on TV, visiting the library or doing research on the computer. Other computer and game time should be significantly limited during school hours to 'break times' only.

## Getting support from your child's school

You may be concerned that your child's school is not going to look kindly on the fact that your child has been missing school. In today's climate there is so much press attention on parents being prosecuted for their children's failure to attend school that parents can feel persecuted and as if they and the school are on opposing sides. It is certainly the case that schools do worry about children who are not in school, and sometimes will need to involve an education welfare officer who is responsible for monitoring and encouraging a child's attendance. However, schools do recognise that children sometimes miss school due to anxiety about attending. We find that schools are generally understanding and helpful if they can see that you are trying to get your child back into school, and they will appreciate your efforts to work with them to get your child back into school full-time.

Schools and education welfare services are very familiar with the principle of children taking a step-by-step approach to returning to school. This must, of course, be negotiated with the school from the start, so you will need to arrange a meeting with your child's teacher, head teacher or head of year, and anyone else involved in monitoring and supporting your child's attendance. At this meeting, discuss the possibility of working out a step-by-step plan with the school. If your child is currently not attending school, this may involve your child gradually building up the amount of time that they spend there.

It is useful to establish whether there is somewhere that your child can go to calm down and where they feel a bit safer in school so that they can withdraw from stress without having to actually leave the school grounds. A resource unit is an excellent place to go to. If your child's school doesn't have one, ask the teacher where else might be a good place. It could simply be the head of year's office or the main office. Having a named person to go to if your child feels anxious can also be important.

It will also be necessary to negotiate how your child gets access to this place or person – for example, if they feel overwhelmed during a lesson and unable to express their concerns to the teacher or in front of the class. Schools are sometimes able to give a child a card that they can present to the teacher, rather than having to speak up, which will allow them time out to calm down at times of high anxiety. Ultimately, we don't want to encourage avoidance, but these strategies can be a useful starting point if it means that your child will be in lessons, even if they leave from time to time, rather than not attending at all. Once they are more comfortable in lessons, it will be important that they are encouraged not to use the card and to try and stay for the whole time.

Another good system is the use of buddies, where the school identifies another pupil who your child can go to for support if they need it, or perhaps meet up with each day to discuss how they are getting on.

The central message behind all of this is that the aim should be gradually to build up your child's attendance with as many systems in place as possible to help them be comfortable staying in school for as long as has been set out in the step-by-step plan. You will achieve this most successfully if you work as a team with your child's school.

## Working as a team with your child's school

1.  Arrange to speak to your child's teacher or head of year as soon as you notice that your child is regularly missing days at school.

2.  Explain why you think your child is anxious about attending school and also ask for the teacher's opinion.

3. Raise any problems that your child has talked to you about at school, such as bullying, so that the school can also start to deal with these.

4. Work with your child and the school to make a step-by-step plan to help your child get back into school.

5. Talk about the possibility of having a safe place or a teacher for your child to go to, or a buddy.

6. Meet regularly with your child's teacher to review progress and iron out any problems with the step-by-step plan.

7. Be positive about your child's school even if you don't think it has handled the situation very well up to now. If you moan about your child's school within earshot of your child, they are even less likely to go back.

8. Be clear with your child that they have to go to school despite the anxieties. Not only does this give the message that avoiding the situation is not an option, but it also shows the school that you are serious about getting your child back to school.

## Should I move my child to a different school?

Often parents who come to our clinics with children who are not attending school ask whether changing schools would be a good idea. Their child is often very keen to move schools as they feel it will solve all the problems.

Children often believe that they won't feel anxious at a new school and that they will make lots of new friends. Unfortunately, changing schools is not always a magic answer and sometimes the same problems occur. As we have said, children who are highly anxious often find attending school hard because they have to separate from you or another carer, answer questions in class, take tests, work in small groups, mix with other children at playtime or cope with what other children might say to them. They will still have to do all these things in a new school.

On the other hand, if your child's fears and worries about school relate to their learning needs not being met, particular children bullying them, feeling that they do not have many friends or don't 'fit in', or they have particular difficulties with the noisy, busy, large environment or ethos of a school, you may feel that moving school is the best thing to do. Some parents simply feel that a particular school is not a good fit with their child's personality or needs. In this situation, a school move may help, but it will be important to research alternative schools carefully and communicate openly with both your child's current school and alternative schools to ensure that the transition is managed effectively by all involved.

Changing schools can be very unsettling for any child as they have to get used to new teachers, new children and a new school layout, and this can cause additional anxiety initially. If you are considering moving your child to a new school, do think about this very carefully and talk to your child's teacher, as well as friends or family members, who might also be able to give you some good advice. The same applies to consideration of home schooling. Talk to people who know your child, and those who have experience of home schooling. Will it allow your child to overcome their anxiety or enable them to avoid addressing it? Will it meet their needs? For example, can you find ways that your child can continue to socialise with their peers, engage in sports, music and other extracurricular activities that are all part of school life or would these opportunities be difficult to arrange?

## What about bullying?

Bullying is something that needs to be tackled. It can involve name-calling, other unpleasant remarks, or physical aggression, such as pushing, hitting or fighting. All schools are required to have an anti-bullying policy. This can typically be found on the school's website and is basically a guide to how they will manage any incidents of bullying within the school. If your child is being bullied, it is important that you talk to the school so that it can deal with it in accordance with its policy. It is important that your child feels that they have some control over what happens as a result of the bullying. Your child should be included in open discussions about how bullying will be handled and they must have the opportunity to discuss any concerns that they have about this so that measures can be taken to resolve these issues.

The first step is that the school is put in a position in which it can look after and take responsibility for your child's best interests. There should be a clear message to your child that bullying is not acceptable, and that definite action needs to be taken. In addition, your child will benefit from making a clear plan of how they should respond to any further bullying incidents. Use the problem-solving strategies described in Chapter 11 to help your child to work out different ways of responding to bullying situations and evaluate which would be the most effective for them.

---

### Key points

- Use questions to find out what your child's anxious expectations are

- Work as a team with your child's school

- Devise a step-by-step plan to help your child get back into school

- Make sure your child's school tackles any bullying issues

- Work with your child to develop solutions to problem situations

# Helping children overcome fears and worries – a guide for teachers

We have written this guide for teachers of children who are experiencing difficulties with anxiety. We hope that it will provide you with a helpful summary of the techniques that parents are using at home so that you can use the same strategies at school. You may well be familiar with some of the ideas already, but if you would like more information about the strategies we have outlined, we suggest you read the rest of the book.

## What are common fears and worries of anxious children?

Everyone, children and adults alike, experiences worries, fears and anxiety some of the time. However, for some children these fears and worries become excessive; they interfere with their everyday life including school attendance and participation in school activities. Fears and worries involve an expectation that something bad is going to happen, our physical responses to this (e.g. 'butterflies' in the tummy, fast breathing, or fast heart rate) and the things we do to keep away from things we fear or to try to stay safe when we have to confront them (e.g. avoiding eye contact in frightening social situations).

Anxiety problems are actually the most common problems in children. Children often do not grow out of these problems, and they can be a risk factor for other issues, such as depression, in adolescence or adulthood. Therefore, it is essential that children experiencing anxiety problems are supported in overcoming their difficulties.

## Fears and worries in school

Children with anxiety difficulties often feel anxious about various aspects of school. There are many different reasons for this. Some children find social situations scary, such as mixing with their peers, speaking to teachers, or contributing in class. Other children are worried about separating from a parent or caregiver. For other children, their worries or anxious expectations are more general and may involve a whole host of different things, including getting told off, not doing well enough in their work or sports, or falling out with a friend. Suffice to say, school can be a scary place for many children. Sometimes you may see the direct effects of this in school – for example, children may be withdrawn, tearful or have behavioural outbursts – but sometimes children may manage to 'keep it together' during the school day and the emotional fallout happens when they get home. This can sometimes lead to a tricky situation for teachers, as parents may be reporting that the child is very anxious about school, but teachers may not see the evidence of that, which may lead them to think the problems are all at home. In these situations, it is really helpful when schools and parents can work together to help the child overcome their difficulties.

# What can be done in school?

There are various things that can be done in school to help children overcome their anxiety difficulties, alongside parents or carers implementing strategies at home. Below we outline strategies that teachers or other school staff we have worked with have found they can use with children to help them to overcome their anxieties.

## *Overcoming fears and worries in school*

We have talked above about the tendency for children to try to stay away from things they are scared of (avoidance) or do things that will make them feel safe (safety behaviours) when they get anxious (such as avoiding eye contact). The trouble is that if anxious children avoid the things that make them feel anxious they don't get the chance to gather new information about the situation, so they don't find out if their anxious expectation will actually happen or not and whether they could really cope.

Here's an example:

*Jane thinks that if she answers a question in class she will get it wrong and her classmates will think that she is stupid. When her teacher asks her a question, she therefore looks down at the desk and does not answer. In doing this, she does not get to know if she would get the answer right, and if she didn't whether her classmates would even care.*

In helping a child overcome their anxieties, the child needs to be supported in gathering new information about their anxious expectations so they can discover that:

1. Things may not turn out as they fear.

2. Even if things don't go well, they can cope or do something about it.

3. By facing fears, we learn new things that help us overcome them.

## Facing fears gradually

When a child is anxious, people around them can often try hard to make sure they won't become distressed. For example:

*Whenever Jane's teacher asked her a question she went red, avoided eye contact and stared at the desk. This seemed to attract more attention to Jane, which the teacher could see was not helping. Gradually she stopped asking Jane questions in the hope that she would begin to put her hand up.*

Although Jane's teacher's response was completely understandable, and in fact showed that she had quite a good understanding of Jane's anxieties, it did also allow Jane to avoid facing her fears and learning from these new experiences. Teachers are in a great position to provide children with opportunities to face their fears gradually so that they can overcome those fears. Here is an example of what Jane's teacher did.

> *Jane's teacher sat down with Jane during break time and let Jane know that he could see she was finding it hard to answer questions. He asked Jane what made it so difficult for her. Jane told him that she was worried that she might get the answer wrong. Jane's teacher suggested they try to find out if she really would get it wrong and what would happen if she did. Every day at break-time he would ask Jane one question from the lesson and they would see how many she got right.*

> *Having done this for a week, Jane and her teacher found that although she didn't always get the answer right she didn't get it wrong more than other children in the class would have done. Her teacher congratulated her. They decided that, as she was so good at answering questions at break time, it was now time to start answering questions in a small group. He agreed that each day when she was working in a small group, he would ask her a*

*question about the work. Jane was worried that she would*
*be singled out, so he agreed to also ask other children in*
*the group questions. Gradually, Jane and her teacher*
*progressed from answering questions individually, to a*
*small group, to the whole class, and finally to asking the*
*teacher a question herself in front of the class.*

## Using problem-solving to tackle real life problems or threats

Although children's anxious expectations are not always realistic, sometimes they might reflect an actual problem that the child is facing. For example, a child who is worried that other children will reject them if they ask to join in because other children are sometimes unkind and say that they don't want to play with them. This will need a different approach. In the case of bullying this clearly needs to be dealt with using official school procedures. However, you may also be able to support the child in problem-solving these types of situations. What can they do if a child says that they do not want to play with them?

Another example might be a child who is worried about doing badly in a test and does in fact struggle academically. You could support the child in problem-solving solutions to this 'real life' problem, thinking with them about things you can be doing at school to help and things they can be doing at home.

## *Tips for helping children to overcome anxiety in school*

In helping children to gather new information about their anxious expectations and to face their fears gradually, the following tips can be useful:

1.  As much as possible, work with the child to set goals so you both know what you want to achieve.

2.  Think about what the child needs to learn in order to challenge their anxious expectations.

3.  Work with the child to develop a plan to test out fears and gain new knowledge. Make a step-by-step plan to gradually try out new things to test their anxious expectations.

4.  If the child struggles with a step, it may simply be too difficult, in which case break it down into smaller ones.

5.  Be open and explicit with parents about the strategies you are using so that you can work together. If a similar approach is being taken at home and at school, change will occur faster. Meet with parent/s to review progress regularly.

6.  Find ways to motivate and reward the child – facing fears is hard work!

7.  Be positive and praise the child – just having a go is an achievement!

8.  Be prepared for setbacks, they always happen. Just try again the next day or the next week.

## *Common concerns*

*If I praise a child who is anxious, won't it just draw more attention to them?*

It is a question of how to give it rather than whether to give it. Negotiate with the child how they would like to receive praise or how they would like to be rewarded. It can be done very subtly, or you can praise them when you meet with them separately or with their parent/s. Similarly, they do not need to be rewarded in front of the whole class if this makes them feel uncomfortable; you can do this away from other pupils if need be.

*I am no expert in children's anxiety, so should I really be doing this type of thing? Is this not more appropriate for a specially trained staff member?*

We would certainly encourage you to work with other members of staff who have particular expertise in helping children with emotional difficulties. However, you are well equipped to help a child in your class: you are likely to know them very well and you will be able to create opportunities for them to face their fears. As long as you communicate regularly with the child and their parent/s, all agree a plan of action and regularly review it together, you are very likely to be helping the child overcome their fears.

*How I am supposed to find the time to do this?*

The strategies described here have all been used by teachers and other school staff that we have worked with. It is true that some extra time and thought may be required to get the ball rolling, but often things can start to change quickly. We would hope that this work will prevent a greater input of time further down the line, should problems become more entrenched. However, there is no reason why you cannot enlist the help of a colleague, perhaps a teaching assistant, specially trained staff member or similar.

# Acknowledgements

We would like to thank all the families that we have worked with – they have taught us so much and have shown us that with motivation and persistence even very severe childhood anxiety problems can be overcome.

We would like to thank all those whose research and clinical practice we have learned from over the years, in particular Ronald Rapee, Jennie Hudson, Vanessa Cobham, Philip Kendall, Jeff Wood, Lynne Murray, Peter Cooper, David Clark and Michelle Craske. Their work has equipped us with a wealth of knowledge and skills that we have applied to our work with children with anxiety problems and subsequently to this book.

We would also like to thank Polly Waite and Peter Cooper for their feedback and support throughout the production of this book, as well as a number of friends and colleagues who generously gave their time to give us feedback on earlier drafts of this book – Brynjar Halldorsson, Harriet Young, Vicki Curry, and Gemma Didcock.

Finally, we would like to thank our own families, Andrew, Jos and Charlie (LW), and Colin, Joe and Ben (CC), for their support and understanding.

# Key references

Rapee, R. M., Abbott, M. J. and Lyneham, H. J. (2006). 'Bibliotherapy for children with anxiety disorders using written materials for parents: A randomized controlled trial'. *Journal of Consulting and Clinical Psychology*, 74(3), 436.

Lyneham, H. J. and Rapee, R. M. (2006). 'Evaluation of therapist-supported parent-implemented CBT for anxiety disorders in rural children'. *Behaviour Research and Therapy*, 44(9), 1287-1300.

Cobham, V. E. (2012). 'Do anxiety-disordered children need to come into the clinic for efficacious treatment?' *Journal of Consulting and Clinical Psychology*, 80(3), 465.

Creswell, C., Violato, M., Fairbanks, H., White, E., Parkinson, M., Abitabile, G., Leidi, A. and Cooper, P. (2017). 'A randomised controlled trial of Brief Guided Parent-delivered Cognitive Behaviour Therapy and Solution Focused Brief Therapy for the treatment of child anxiety disorders: Clinical outcome and cost-effectiveness'. *The Lancet Psychiatry*, 4(7), 529-539.

Hill, C., Waite, P. and Creswell, C. (2016) 'Anxiety disorders in children and adolescents'. *Paediatrics and Child Health, 26(12), 548-553.*

Thirlwall, K., Cooper, P., Karalus, J., Voysey, M., Willetts, L. and Creswell, C. (2013) 'Treatment of childhood anxiety disorders via guided parent-delivered cognitive behavioural therapy: A randomised controlled trial'. *British Journal of Psychiatry,* 203(6), 436-444.

Waters, A. M., Ford, L. A., Wharton, T. A. and Cobham, V. E. (2009). 'Cognitive-behavioural therapy for young children with anxiety disorders: Comparison of a child + parent condition versus a parent only condition'. *Behaviour Research and Therapy,* 47(8), 654-662.

# Useful resources

Bryon, Mandy, and Titman, Penny, *Helping Your Child with a Physical Health Condition* (Robinson, 2019)

Butler, Gillian, *Overcoming Social Anxiety and Shyness, 2nd Edition: A self-help guide using cognitive behavioural techniques*, (Robinson, 2016)

Chellingsworth, Marie, and Farrand, Paul, *How to Beat Worry and Generalised Anxiety Disorder One Step at a Time* (Robinson, 2016)

Dunsmuir, Sandra, Dewey, Jessica, and Birch, Susan, *Helping Your Child with Friendship Problems* (Robinson, 2019)

Hiller, Rachel, and Gradisar, Michael, *Helping Your Child with Sleep Problems* (Robinson, 2018)

Hogan, Brenda, and Brosan, Lee, *An Introduction to Coping with Anxiety*, 2nd edition (Robinson, 2018)

Kennerley, Helen, *Overcoming Anxiety*, 2nd edition (Robinson, 2014)

Meares, Kevin, and Freeston, Mark, *Overcoming Worry*, 2nd edition (Robinson, 2015)

Parkinson, Monica, and Reynolds, Shirley, *Teenage Depression* (Robinson, 2015)

Reynolds, Shirley, and Parkinson, Monica, *Am I Depressed and What Can I Do About It?* (Robinson, 2015)

# Index

Note: page numbers in **bold** refer to diagrams.

16 Helping Your Child with Fears and Worries

# THE
# IMPR⟳VEMENT
# ZONE

## Looking for life inspiration?

The Improvement Zone has it all, from **expert advice** on how to advance your **career** and boost your **business**, to improving your **relationships**, revitalising your **health** and developing your **mind**.

Whatever your goals, head to our website now.

www.improvementzone.co.uk

INSPIRATION ON THE MOVE

INSPIRATION DIRECT TO YOUR INBOX